HEART PEACE

Embracing Life's Adversities

ADOLFO QUEZADA

Foreword by
Fr. William Burke

Resurrection Press
An Imprint of
CATHOLIC BOOK PUBLISHING CO.
Totowa • New Jersey

To my father and my mother

Published in 1999 by Resurrection Press, Ltd.
P.O. Box 248
Williston Park, NY 11596

Copyright © Adolfo Quezada

ISBN 1-878718-52-5

Library of Congress Catalog Card Number 99-70150

Cover design and cover photo by John Murello

Printed in Canada.

    2   3   4   5   6   7   8   9

Contents

Foreword

SOMETIMES, WHEN I AM READING A BOOK that offers advice about living with physical or emotional pain, I come to a "crossroads" — a place at which I decide whether or not I will go on reading.

Such a fork in the road came when I was reading *Heart Peace*, and I reached this observation from Adolfo Quezada:

When we give our depression respect and attention, we allow ourselves to learn from it what we must learn.

As a person who lives with chronic depression, I don't take such advice easily, if at all. I look for credentials first. Does this author know anything about depression or any other serious pain...from within? Is this a writer who is him, or herself, a "wounded healer"? Or am I being offered merely pious suggestion, flippant counsel from one with no *real* experience?

I moved past my crossroads in *Heart Peace* and went on reading. For as you yourself will discover, Adolfo

Quezada is the real thing, a truly perceptive guide through the torments which can make life a hell. He has been there, into deep suffering, and emerged from it with great wisdom.

As he says:

How ironic that the only path toward integration is disintegration. How paradoxical that the gateway to heaven is hell itself.

To try to learn anything from serious suffering while we are going through it, is — to say the least — a monumental challenge. Usually we want only for the pain to go away. We don't want a lesson, we want a way out.

But Adolfo Quezada suggests that when we don't try to learn from our pain, we risk that pain becoming truly worth-less. In some way, we must "embrace" our suffering, we must look behind the mask of The Beast to see what truth lies there. That truth, as Quezada notes, can be liberating:

The attitude we choose toward our suffering can transcend the suffering itself, and create something good out of something bad.

Incredibly, and constantly, that is true. I have learned it in my own life and from the living testimony of family and friends who have suffered far more than myself. Each Sunday of the Easter season, when, as celebrant of the liturgy, I proclaim "the Paschal Mystery" — the victory of life *through* suffering — I see that victory in the faces of so many people in front of me. Their suffering has shaped them into splendid human beings.

Nevertheless, to achieve such a victory remains a challenge, and it is always a hard and weary fight. When the pain is bad, a triumph of any kind can seem impossible.

Let this gentle and persuasive book give you new hope. More is happening in our suffering than we know. For one thing, the Divine Beloved, who has himself been in agony, is aware of our agony, and bears it with us. As Quezada notes,

> *Sometimes all we need is for our suffering to be acknowledged by someone who accepts it. Sometimes all we need is for someone to cry with us.*

And when that Someone is the one who wept for Lazarus, we know nothing can finally defeat us.

FR. BILL BURKE

Preface

PERHAPS YOU ARE FEELING MUCH ANGUISH and despair right now. You may be experiencing a very difficult time at work, or you may be involved in an unhappy relationship. You may be facing a crippling or terminal illness; you may be dreading the consequences of mistakes you have made; or you may be in physical or psychic pain. You may be feeling the excruciating pain of loneliness, the fear of abandonment, or the insecurity of the unknown. You want to live, but life hurts too much to go on. You want peace so badly, but all you seem to experience is misery. The whole world appears dark and menacing. Your internal wound is great and the bleeding doesn't seem to stop. The tears you shed are as constant as the pain from which they come. All of these are important feelings that you are experiencing and at times they must seem overwhelming to you. There seems to be no way out of this, but please believe me, there is.

There has been no darker time for me than when my son was killed. The years that have passed since that dreadful time have been full of an agony too great to bear, and yet, I have borne it. They have included days in which I did not want to live, and yet, I have lived through it. At the time I truly believed that such a loss was a wound too deep to heal, and yet, I have been healing. The journey through desolation is long and arduous, but we do not make it alone.

I believe that God cries with us, mourns our losses, and suffers our pain. God is with us always, even when it does not appear so. And God is unconditionally forgiving. Because God loves you so much, God would have you live life fully. You can work through these difficult times with the help of God. When life is out of control and completely without meaning, then you are ready to receive God's help. You have nothing to lose and everything to gain. With God working through you, life becomes manageable again, little by little.

It is here, at the point of annihilation that you can save your soul. Out of our hopelessness, the hope of God prevails. From behind the wall of your shame-filled self, your secrets are set free. As your false self dies off, your true self is born anew. As you face your fear, you are given courage; as you acknowledge your brokenness, you are healed. The long, dark night now breaks into the promise of tomorrow.

Life is a tornado. It is a whirlwind that tosses and turns you, lifts you to the heavens and crashes you into the rocks, and, at the same time, at the center of it all, there is a peace that surpasses all understanding. It is a stillness that calls the deep within you to the deep that is God. This is the nature of life. When you least expect it, you are torn from that quiet place and thrown into the strife. And, when you least expect it, you discover the eye of the storm in the midst of the tornado.

As a child of God you are called to love: love of God, love of self, and love of others. It is a love that sustains you through the darkest of nights. As a child of God you can see time through the eyes of eternity. As a child of God you are invited to rest from time to time. As a child of God you are encouraged to live in such a way that you honor your physical self. As a child of God you abandon your quest for perfection, and embrace your imperfection humbly and gratefully. As a child of God you are beckoned to be one with God in prayer and meditation, there to discover that, even in the worst of times, God is with you.

Regardless of the conditions or the circumstances of your life, if you believe God is with you, hope springs eternal. Your hope, then, transcends what is before you, not by thinking about tomorrow, but by daring to stay in the present and finding God's love in the eternal now.

1

Why the Suffering?

SOMETIMES LIFE IS MORE *than we can bear. We are bent down under the weight of our troubles and broken by the impact of our suffering. We try to understand the mystery of suffering but to no avail. With arms extended toward the heavens we ask, "Why?" half-way expecting an answer, but we know there will be no answer, no reason given for what is happening to us. We want to understand our suffering so we can control it, yet we never completely understand, and our frustration only compounds our suffering. Ultimately, we come to realize that suffering is a part of life, and that if it is to make any sense or logic, we will have to be the ones to give our suffering a sense of meaning and purpose by the way we embrace life's adversities.*

The Cause of Suffering

Sometimes we can see a direct correlation between our actions and our suffering, but a direct cause and effect connection is not always clear. Often our suffering is brought on by the actions of others, by heredity, destructive acts of nature, or accidents. Bad things happen to us in life whether we deserve them or not. They just happen.

We are sorely disappointed when we suffer even after we have obeyed the "rules" that were supposed to keep us safe and sound. We discover, eventually, that there are no guarantees against suffering, regardless of how we have lived our life. It seems so unfair to us to see that some people who have not obeyed the "rules" are apparently free of suffering, while others who have observed the rules are not spared from suffering. Just like the rain that falls on the just and the unjust, suffering respects no person and recognizes no boundary.

In our attempt to make some sense of our suffering we sometimes look for a culprit, a cause, a source of our suffering. Sometimes we blame God. God must be punishing us for our wrongdoing, we reason, because otherwise an all-benevolent God would not allow suffering. But even in God's goodness God cannot stop the suffering that comes with living, neither can God direct the suffering toward the bad and away from the good. God does not will suffering for us; God wills that we live and love and embrace life and all that comes with it, including ecstasy and joy, pain and suffering.

When we talk about suffering we are really talking about living and loving, giving and receiving. We don't have to go seeking after suffering. As we dare to live and love, give and receive, suffering finds us.

There is no virtue in suffering. Whenever it is possible to prevent suffering for ourselves or others, or to alleviate it, or bring it to an end, we are compelled by love to do so. It is only when it is clear that our suffering cannot be avoided that we forsake our resistance and enter into it with our whole selves, and thereby transform it into a life-giving force for life.

Entering into Suffering

When our suffering has been traumatic and prolonged we sometimes react to it by withdrawing from life in self-protection. Whether our suffering happened in the past or is happening now, it has had a profound effect on how we interact with the world and with ourselves. Our natural tendency is to brace ourselves against life in order to avoid being hurt again. We numb ourselves out by becoming overly involved in activity, by dissociation, by using drugs, and by entering into impossible relationships. Ironically, it is when we refuse to live and love in an attempt to avoid further suffering, that we suffer most of all. There is no worse hell than refusing to live fully for fear of experiencing the suffering that comes with life.

We have been urged to rise above our suffering, but in our suffering we soon discover that the only way to get beyond our pain is to go into it and through it. Our suffering can be the ashes from which new life emerges, but first, we experience the suffering; we enter into the fire. We are called to open our whole being to the experiences of life, including the suffering, and then respond to it. When we close ourselves to our suffering, we close ourselves to everything. When we open to our suffering, we open to all. We enter into our suffering not as victims being led to the slaughter, but as courageous survivors whose core is beyond the reach of pain, suffering, and even death.

We come to respect and understand our suffering, to listen to it, to learn from it, and to allow ourselves to be transformed by it. Suffering has a way of shaking us loose from our attachment to the temporal. We change our perceptions and rearrange our priorities. Suffering keeps us caring. When we listen to our suffering we learn just how powerless we are in life, and we discover just how little control we have over our own destiny. When we allow it, our suffering can bring us to a deeper awareness of our life and the lives of others. Whether we like it or not, our suffering awakens us from a slumber of apathy and moves us toward a state of being fully alive. Suffering tempers us and prepares us for even more suffering in the days ahead. Above all, through our suffering, we can learn to let go of some things. As we respond to our suffering and the suffering of others, we grow in strength and maturity. Fulfillment in life comes in many ways through our suffering. Nothing is the same on the other side of suffering.

As we face a particularly difficult or painful part of our life, we may need to go off into our own "Garden of Gethsemane" to prepare ourselves for what is to come. Here, we can wail and plead; here, we can bargain and cajole; here, we can demand our own will; here, we can accept what is, and receive the comfort of God as we walk forward into what must be.

In the face of suffering we encounter our weaknesses. This is a time to be patient with ourselves, not judgmental or critical. By humbly allowing for our weaknesses we can better defend against them. Intolerance to our weaknesses gives them the control. What we need most from ourselves now is forgiveness and encouragement. We remember that in our weakness is our strength to heal.

Facing Emotions

We may feel hurt, helpless, guilty, confused, angry, overwhelmed, sad, anxious, frustrated, depressed, afraid, bereaved, or other devastating emotions. We don't have to judge or suppress our feelings; we can give them expression as we tell our story. We can tell our story to someone whom we trust to listen and care without prejudice, but when there is no one to tell, we can tell our story to a journal; we can tell our story to

God in prayer; and we can tell our story through the creative expression of our art. There is healing in the act of expression.

The help we receive when we share our burden with others is not the elimination of our suffering, but the acceptance it. Others, who have also suffered, know only too well what we are experiencing and they can enter into our suffering with us, even though they cannot take away our pain. Sometimes all we need is for our suffering to be acknowledged by someone who accepts it. Sometimes all we need is for someone to cry with us.

When our suffering results from the actions or inactions of others, it is filled with anger toward our perpetrators. When we acknowledge our anger and give it constructive expression, it lessens to a level that does not interfere with our full engagement with our suffering. Forgiveness of our perpetrators comes only after we have dealt fully with our anger toward them. Then, forgiveness can take the sting out of our suffering.

When our suffering is clearly a direct consequence of our own action or inaction we do not ask, "Why did this happen to me?" but we suffer just the same. Usually, this kind of suffering is compounded with a sense of guilt. Forgiving ourselves for our error helps us to better cope with the suffering that comes in its wake. Here, mercy becomes our ally in healing.

Our fear of suffering can cause us to become self-centered. It may preoccupy us with ourselves to the exclusion of others. Our fear of suffering can cause us more harm than the suffering itself. Our fear is legitimate and understandable and need not be eliminated, but in order to live fully, we tap the courage within us and move ahead in spite of our fear. Our experience of dealing with suffering enables us to put it into perspective and lessens our fear of it.

Invoking the Spirit

Suffering is powerful and can immobilize us. It can absolutely overwhelm our faith. When we are in the midst of our suffering it is nearly impossible to maintain strong faith. This is a time when we begin to lose hope. As despair sets in we begin to doubt that God is there for us; we feel forsaken and we don't know where to turn.

Suffering can also be faith-building. Even as we face our suffering, we can cling to the belief that, although God may not rescue us from our suffering, God has already provided us with all we need to deal with it. Our hope is not that the suffering cease, although that would be welcomed, rather, it is that we will be able to deal with whatever suffering comes. Our faith is not that everything will be all right, because it may not be, but that, no matter what happens, God will be with us and will comfort us. The comfort and hope that is given is strength, energy, and spirit.

Our suffering has a way of turning our attention from the external in our life to the internal. Matters of the spirit become more important than they have ever been, and we begin to opt for the eternal over the temporal.

We are not called to martyrdom, rather, we are called to be faithful through the pain and not to despair. Through our suffering we can discover a faith we didn't know we had. Through our suffering we can draw closer to God. Through our suffering we can be transformed so that we are still in the world but not of it. When we are willing to live and love, even after we have suffered, we are being faithful to God and to life itself.

At the height of our suffering we are tempted to pray that this cup pass us by. We want to ask for relief from our agony and deliverance from our misery, yet, to pray for the elimination of our suffering we would have to believe that God is causing it and therefore can also stop it if we can only talk him into it. While God's grace does not rescue us from the consequences of our behavior or the effects of our misfortune, it does give us the wherewithal to deal with our suffering in such a way that we learn and grow from it. Without grace it is impossible for us to deal with our suffering.

When we pray it is not to anesthetize ourselves against the pain of life. In fact, prayer helps us to touch the reality of our life, including pain and suffering. In prayer we receive the insight of how all things can work for the sake of God's purpose, even pain and suffering, even death.

Our prayer is not a means to an end, but the end itself. When we pray we are communing with God; we are allowing the essence of God to flow within us and to impact on our life. This is the purpose of our life, to be one with God, and to let God love through us in the world. Our prayer does not change God and perhaps not even the circumstances in which we suffer, but it does change us and the way we respond to and cope with our suffering. When we pray we use the gifts we have been given from the beginning: courage, strength, and spirit. When we pray we invoke the compassion of God and God enters into our suffering with us and shares our pain. When we pray we are not alone.

In the midst of our suffering we are hard pressed to feel loving to anyone, least of all God. Yet, it is here, in the darkest hour of our life that we are capable of loving God the most. To love God because God can rescue us from our suffering is to love God's power, not God. To love God, even when God appears powerless to help us, is to love God for God's sake alone. In our love for God we yearn for God's presence. We manifest our love for God by acknowledging the divine presence with us even in our suffering. God is one with us. God feels our ecstasy and our agony. Believing that God is with us, no matter what happens to us is what gives us the courage, the heart, and the spirit to persevere and overcome our suffering.

God loves us unconditionally. The will of God is not that we suffer, but rather, that we live life in its fullest sense. Suffering is an integral part of life and when we accept life we accept the suffering that comes with it. But God does not abandon us in our suffering. God is here with us, even in our most difficult hour. God is not a Divine Magician who makes our suffering disappear; God is the Divine Lover who remains to suffer with us and stays with us forever. God is the courage that propels us and the strength with which we endure. God is the faith that motivates us and the love that carries us. We believe in God in the good times, but we come to know God in the bad. Our suffering is God's suffering, and we are bonded at the soul.

Giving Meaning and Purpose

Connected to the grace of God through prayer we are less apt to despair. In fact, our attitude may change dramatically. In tune with the spirit, we may change our whole perspective toward our suffering. Where before we might be helpless prisoners of life, we can now free ourselves regardless of what is happening to us. Our freedom is our ability to respond to life, including our suffering, any way we choose. The attitude we choose toward our suffering can transcend the suffering itself and create something good out of something bad. We can choose to give meaning to our suffering and purpose to our life. Through prayer, that is, listening to the God within, and by waiting in faith, the significance of our suffering is made clear to us.

We may be forced to let go of the dreams we had for ourselves; we may be forced to let go of life as we would have preferred it; but we do not have to let go of that indestructible inner force from which we get solace, hope, and purpose to go on living. This is the precious gift of hope kept alive in our human spirit.

By finding meaning in our suffering we can transcend it. We can decide that even our suffering will serve God. We can let our suffering teach us an important lesson that we otherwise would not have learned. We can dedicate our suffering to God, to another person, or to a cause in which we believe. We can endure and even overcome our suffering when there is a reason for it.

Why the suffering? It may come to us because of one reason, but we can give it another. While bad things do not happen to us in order that good can come of them, we can choose to let good things come of them. We can give constructive purpose even to the most destructive of circumstances. The question becomes not, what suffering will come to us, but what stand we will take toward it. Whether by accident or by the cruelty of others, suffering comes our way, yet all the misfortune in life or the ill-will of humanity cannot penetrate the sanctuary of our soul. It is here that we take our stand. It is here that we take courage. It is here that we overcome the world.

Integrating Love

Because we understand how devastating suffering can be, we undertake the mission to alleviate it among those who live in our world. Our heart breaks for those in pain. It is as though their suffering bonds us with them. Sometimes we are tempted to separate from those who suffer because we are unable to help them and we feel inadequate and helpless. When we dare to stay and embrace the suffering, we may find ways in which we can help after all. Always we can have compassion for them, that is, we can connect with their suffering, even when we cannot alleviate it. We suffer and we heal, and because we have suffered, we can be healers.

We can acknowledge suffering as a very real and vital part of life; we can trace it to its source; we can cooperate with it, and direct it toward the purposes of God. Suffering need not be a cage for us, but it can be an expansion into abundant life. Although our suffering is sometimes overbearing, we do not have to focus our whole attention on it. Instead, we can focus on our need to love, and discover that an integral part of loving is suffering. Unless we integrate our suffering with our love, it is a total waste. Ultimately, it is our love that redeems suffering.

God of the Suffering

Why, God, must we be broken before we can be whole? Why must the darkness come before the light? Why must we face death before we enter into life? It seems so futile sometimes to go on living in the face of affliction and struggle. How ironic that the only path toward integration is disintegration. How paradoxical that the gateway to heaven is hell itself.

We are forced by the traumatic events and circumstances of our life to stop and look at ourselves. We are compelled by the accidents and misfortunes that come our way to slow our pace and re-evaluate what is really important to us. Sometimes our ruptured life becomes an opportunity to learn and grow. Even illness and the imminence of death can awaken us to meaningful living.

We turn to you, not for consolation, but for sustenance; not to be rescued, but transformed; not for restoration, but new life.

We live life and we experience abandonment, helplessness, and despair. We believe in you, who love us beyond our comprehension; you, who enter into our abandonment, share our impotence, and understand our desperation. Only you, who are revealed in the authenticity of life, including suffering, is real to us.

You stay with us even through the darkest of nights. You are a vulnerable God who enters into the fire and dies with us. Here, at the confluence of life and death, our opposites are reconciled. Our shattered forces are gathered, and our oneness with you is revealed. This is all that really matters.

2

Sacred Anxiety

DIVINE BELOVED, *you infuse us with sacred
anxiety of the heart. We are left seeking,
yearning, pining for that which was and can
again be ours.
In sacred anxiety we are conscious of a
desperate emptiness which only you can fill. We
are aware of a painful poverty which only you
can take away. We feel an insatiable hunger and
thirst which only you can satisfy.
It is a fear, a dread, a terror deep within that we
will not see you before us, hear you in our heart,
and sense your presence in our midst.
In sacred anxiety we dare not leave the present
moment, for here is where we rendezvous. Here
is where you touch our soul and animate our spirit.
We come to know you, Divine Beloved, as we
breathe into our body the Life that is yours, and
breathe out in trusting self-surrender. We know*

you in our stillness, in our silence,
and in our thoughtlessness.
Though our world be shattered and our life
be torn apart, we know you in the dark and deep
where we come to rest in you.

The Face of Anxiety

Anxiety is an intangible. It comes over us like an all-pervasive feeling of danger, but we know not the exact nature of the danger. There is also a sense of helplessness in anxiety because we don't know exactly how to defend ourselves against the unknown threat. We can stand to face a known threat, but what we don't know is harder to deal with. So the fear of an unknown threat to our well-being is the anxiety we experience.

In our anxiety we feel much confusion and ambiguity. Things are not clear. If they were, then our anxiety would not be anxiety, it would be fear. Fear is our response to a clear and present danger. We respond to our fear with the fight-or-flight reaction in which our body is filled with adrenaline and prepares to confront or flee from the perceived threat. Our anxiety is more a dread of a hidden peril. While fear is the response we may have to a more immediate threat, anxiety is usually based on future events.

We need to expose what it is that we are afraid of. Bringing it into the light we can better determine how to proceed against it. When we know the size and strength of the enemy we can prepare our resources.

Anxiety is often rooted in our history. Some of us were raised in dysfunctional families which were bastions of chaos and anxiety. It may be that we lived in an alcoholic home or were raised by parents on whom we could not depend. The experience of uncertainty during our childhood may have contributed to our propensity toward anxiety. Not knowing what to expect day to day as children, contributes greatly to anxiety in adulthood.

Anxiety is often connected to an actual major loss or the threat of such a loss. A death in the family, an experience of abuse, a separation from a close friend, a divorce, any of these may be the source of unresolved grief that results in symptoms of anxiety.

Our anxiety is sometimes tied to losing something to which we cling. When we release our hold on it, when we set it free from us, we are also set free from it and from our anxiety. In reality, we have nothing to lose. This is the peace of poverty. "Blessed are the poor in spirit, for theirs is the kingdom of heaven" (Mt 5:3).

Letting go of our illusion of control over that which we have absolutely no control is perhaps one of the most difficult tasks before us, yet, this release is a major factor in any anxiety reduction we may hope to experience.

Even as we begin to release our hold on the illusion of control, our anxiety begins to abate. It seems that in our desperate attempt to avoid the sense of helplessness, we conjure up ways in which we believe we have some control. The reality is that we have little or no control over much of what happens in our lives and the lives of others, But it is not a matter of giving in to the forces which work against us or of becoming perpetual victims. Rather, our task is to determine realistically that over which we have some control and that over which we have none. Letting go of that over which we have no control frees us to focus all of our resources on that over which we have some control, namely ourselves.

The willingness to stop trying to control people or circumstances to meet our expectations or desires can be a giant step toward heart peace. As long as we believe we can exert control over others or over what is going to happen tomorrow, we live in a constant state of anxiety. When we realize that we can only control how we respond to what comes, our anxiety level drops dramatically.

There is much we can do today to affect what will happen tomorrow, but this is a far cry from controlling the future. It is not sufficient just to let go of our control over tomorrow or over future events. We must also cling to a faith that lets us believe in ourselves now. We come to believe that whatever happens, we will handle it. We have been given all that we need to respond to life as it unfolds before us. As long as we confront one moment at a time we can handle it. It is only when we take on more than the moment at hand that we become anxious and overwhelmed. The faith to which we hold can also provide us with the inner certitude that what we cannot handle, God can and will. We are to help ourselves, to be sure, but we will not be abandoned to face our difficulties alone. Such a faith diminishes our level of anxiety.

Much of our anxiety comes as a result of duality.

That is, we allow our minds to be divided between competing interests. On the one hand we want to be living one way, and on the other hand, we want to be living another. We want to be God-conscious, yet, our minds take us to places and things which separate us from God. We are told in scripture that no one can serve two masters. Through prayer and meditation we become single-minded and disallow the duality that steals our peace away. To be single-minded does not mean to be closed-minded. On the contrary, when our mind is dedicated to the law of love, we are opened to many possibilities, but our pursuit of these is based on the one thing necessary, the way of God. Scripture admonishes us, "...you are anxious and troubled about so many things, and yet few are needed, indeed only one," (Lk 10:38). To be single-minded is to be pure in heart, to be pure in heart is to practice the presence of God in our lives constantly and unceasingly. "Blessed are the pure of heart, for they shall see God" (Mt 5:8).

The anticipation that things may not turn out the way we want or having unrealistic expectations may result in anxiety. We are probably all perfectionists in one sense or another, so it is important to be aware of how that shapes our life. Settling for too little can be stressful and therefore anxiety-provoking, but settling for nothing but the best or nothing less than 100% is usually unattainable and an invitation to anxiety.

We have been conditioned to move as fast as we can in order to accomplish as much as we can in the shortest amount of time. Our hurry-up environment creates an atmosphere of chaos and agitation. It is a way of life that breeds anxiety. Slowing down our mind, our body, and our life brings more clarity, more efficiency, more appreciation of what is. "The butterfly counts not months but moments and has time enough" (Rabindranath Tagore).

Some of us feel as though we are in a constant state of incompleteness. Our attempt to find that which would complete us contributes to our anxiety. After much searching and knocking, we often discover that what we believed was missing was with us all along. What matters most is appreciating what we have and using it to its greatest potential. We are animated and find heart peace when our mission in life is based on what we have available to work with. To set unrealistic goals and expectations not only frustrates us, but programs us to fail and provokes our anxiety. "You have made us for Yourself and our hearts are restless until they rest in You" (St. Augustine).

To be or not to be is a subject of great anxiety, existential anxiety. To cease being altogether is frightening to us at a deep level, and not knowing what our fate will be is a source of ongoing anxiety. The antidote to existential anxiety is our love of the Divine. We don't know the nature of our union with heaven, yet we come to believe that it is real and sublime. It is this love affair with God that overcomes any fear or anxiety we may have about dying before we die. The power of our divine communion also allays our anxiety about physical death. Our anxiety becomes a kind of anxiousness. We are anxious to be with our Divine Beloved. Ours is a sacred anxiety. "Were I to come to the end I would still be with you"(Ps 139:18).

Responding to Anxiety

It is all right to be anxious. In fact, the first step in responding to our anxiety is to acknowledge it and allow it to be without judgment. Let us not fall into the temptation of trying to do away with our anxiety. Let us embrace it and let it prompt movement in our lives.

In our search for serenity we must not attempt to rid ourselves permanently of anxiety, for anxiety is a friend that can also warn us of impending danger. Rather, we need to acknowledge our anxiety and listen to what it is trying to tell us about our lives. Serenity is the result of the transformation of anxiety into faith.

We can use our anxiety to give us the energy we need to confront and overcome the difficulties of life. Giving purpose to our anxiety makes it more manageable and useful.

People, things, and circumstances matter to us and when they are threatened something within us sounds an alarm. Our body goes into a state of arousal. We are ready to protect ourselves against the real or imagined threat.

To stay conscious to the moment before us is perhaps the greatest gift we can give to God. It is, after all, a sign of love to be wakeful and attentive to life, and appreciative of that which God lays before us moment by moment.

Mindful living comes easily to a child. She is not worrying about tomorrow and she is not lamenting yesterday. She is watching the lady bug crawling on a twig; she is relishing every lick of her lollipop; she is listening intently to the sounds of the world; she is deeply involved with the feel of soft green grass between her bare toes. She is wakefully living the eternal moment.

How easily we are lured away from the now as we forget our childlike nature. It is like leaving the eye of the tornado. Quickly we are whirled away by the storm of anxiety, and are caught up in the vicious cycle of obsession. Only by returning to the center of the storm, the core of who we are, can we return to mindful living and serenity.

The gift of life is in the moment at hand. But it is one thing to talk about living in the present moment and quite another to actually do it. We have been taught to leave the reality of the present and enter into the illusion of the future. We are accustomed to living in a perpetual trance that offers us neither here nor there, but only an anxiety-producing limbo.

The peace that surpasses all understanding is the peace that comes to us when we stop trying to figure out what is going to happen to us, when we stop looking anywhere except right in front of us. To do this requires tremendous courage because it is very frightening to let go of our illusion of control. The truth is that as long as we are not living in the here and now, as long as our minds are somewhere else, worrying about tomorrow, we are definitely not in control. It is only when we return to the only reality, which is the now, that we can gain some control.

There are times when it is easy to let our minds wander. Because we are idle as we wait in line at the grocery store does not mean that we should cease to live fully. Wherever we are and regardless of the circumstances, we have it in our power to become actively aware of our surroundings, our circumstances, and our current reality. Returning our mind to the present is not as difficult as keeping it there. Our mind is like a bird that would prefer to fly all around considering the possibilities than to land and survey the ground where it lives now.

Only by remaining in the present moment can we influence the future. It is in the present that we can affect how the past impacts on us, and it is in the present that we will affect what the future will be. We can cherish our yesterday and we can anticipate tomorrow, but the moment before us is the crux of our reality. We are afraid to live in the present because it feels stifling and limiting. But life is the moment at hand, all else is memory or imagination. Our task is to take what is before us and break it down into bite-size portions that we can chew and swallow without choking.

One way to remain in the present moment is to allow thoughts to drop from our mind like petals off a flower. Thoughts usually provoke emotions which also are not our true selves. Thoughts can be acknowledged, appreciated, and then released. Thoughts only get in the way of the practice of the present. It isn't only negative thoughts that rob us of the eternal now, it may also be positive thoughts, thoughts of good things to come. We can save ourselves many anxious moments by dropping thoughts even as they come, and daring to stay in what is right now.

There are specific actions we can take to bring ourselves back into the present moment and stay there, if only for a little while. One way to practice presence is to use our senses to connect with our present reality. We look at our shoes and acknowledge them as shoes. We hear the song of a bird and become actively aware of it. We allow the taste of a delicious morsel to fill our awareness. We feel the keys of the computer giving way under the creative movement of our fingers.

Staying in the present moment has to do with openness. We see the beauty or the ugliness that is before us. We hear the sounds that happen around us. We taste the myriad experiences of the mouth. We smell the aroma that dominates our space. We touch and allow the sensations of life to be visited upon us. Our mind opens to what is, and our heart invites the immediate, yet infinite presence of God.

When we pay attention to the moment at hand we bring to it the benefit of our full consciousness. This is the moment in which we love. This is the moment in which we are loved. Love by its nature is neither in

the past nor in the future, only in the now. Life is here.
Life is now. Where are we?

In the present moment we face our poverty, and we
are compelled to be honest about ourselves. When we
dare to remain in the present moment we make ourselves available to God. Staying in the present
moment we learn to be dependent on God and to trust
in that over which we have no control.

Our responsibility is to take the present and love it
fully. We cannot possess the moment, but we can fill
it with love before we commend it to eternity.

If a sense of security and safety works to relieve our
anxiety, then what is it that provides such security and
safety to us? Where can we look to for this protection
except God? Scripture tells us to, "Have no anxiety
about anything, but in everything by prayer and supplication with thanksgiving let your requests be made
known to God..." From this comes "...the peace of
God, which passes all understanding..." (Phil 4:1-7).

Scripture tells us not to be anxious about what we
will eat or drink or about what we will wear. Life is
more important than the material things we need or
want. God takes care of nature, will we not also be
cared for? Our anxiety can change nothing, our faith
in God and in ourselves can. We are asked to put all
of our attention, all of our psychic energy into seeking
the spiritual realm within us from which emanates all
that we need. Seek first the realm of God and the
righteousness of heaven, and everything else that you
need will be given you. "Therefore do not be anxious

about tomorrow, for tomorrow will be anxious for itself. Let the day's own trouble be sufficient for the day" (Mt 6:34).

Transforming Anxiety

Because we breathe automatically we can do so even in a trance. But conscious breathing compels us to acknowledge the present. Our breath can anchor the ship that is our mind in the stormy sea that is our life. It can be a gentle summons to return to the sobriety of the now. Nothing is as vital to our life as our breath, yet we easily forget it. Remembering our breath, we remember ourselves.

We can use the rhythmic in and out breathing of our body to center us and release tension and anxiety. Each breath brings us into the present where there is no anxiety, no hold on the past or future. Breathing in and breathing out we return to the reality of the now.

As we allow ourselves to be who we were created to be, we can allow the feelings that come to be experienced and expressed. All of our feelings are valid and real and need not be censored or avoided. There is a direct connection between suppression of emotions and anxiety.

Dare we be kind to ourselves? What we say to ourselves matters so much. We have the power through our self-talk to encourage or discourage ourselves. We can calm or agitate our heart. We can raise or lower our self-esteem. The first step is to be aware of the words we use and the approach we take in our inner dialogue. Self-talk can include reassurance and hope — these are antidotes to anxiety.

As we take care of ourselves in general, we take care of our anxiety in particular. Our anxiety is exacerbated when we are fatigued or otherwise not feeling well. Lack of adequate sleep and exercise and improper diet, lead to a low-grade depression and anxiety. The better we feel physically, the better we feel emotionally. When our physical system is out of order it begins a vicious cycle that is hard to break. For example, lack of sleep results in anxiety about day-to-day matters. Our anxiety then keeps us from getting proper sleep, and so it goes. The same holds for diet and exercise.

If the anxiety we feel is an acute sense of groundlessness, then it makes sense that finding our true ground of being, God alone, brings us heart peace. "The Lord is my light and my salvation; whom shall I fear? The Lord is the stronghold of my life; of whom shall I be afraid?" (Ps 27:1).

Love is stronger than the clutch of anxiety. It is the power of love that breaks the stronghold of our fear of the unknown. The influence of love is such that it opens us to life and to all that comes with it. Love enables us to believe in what we cannot see or feel. It lets us move with the confidence of knowing even when we don't. Love gives us the courage to proceed even in the face of great anxiety. "Peace! Be Still! And the wind ceased, and there was a great calm" (Mk 4:39).

Scripture tells us not to fear those who can kill the body but nothing else. Instead, we are to fear any force that can keep us trapped and separated from God. In the face of anxiety we are encouraged to remember how important we are in the realm of life. If tiny sparrows are remembered by God, and even the hairs on our head are numbered, how much more valuable are we in the eye of God. The peace that comes, even through our anxiety, is a peace that is rooted in the heart knowledge that we are loved profoundly by all that is God.

Heart peace is not a state of bliss that is completely untouched by anxiety. Anxiety needs to be balanced with the other emotions that come, especially those emotions which may be calming to us. We allow heart peace by seeking balance in our lives. That is, allowing the yin and yang energies each to have their impact on us. The yin energy allows our nervous system to calm down and heal. The yang energy enables us to move into action and get things done. The two energies do not work against each other, but are complementary and each perpetuates the life of the other. Even our breath includes yin and yang. We breath in and are gifted with life; we breathe out and make our contribution to the world. Inhaling we receive; exhaling we give.

As we respond to anxiety we must accept responsibility for our lives and seek necessary changes in our way of living and our behavior. "...you know what hour it is, how it is full time now for you to wake from sleep...let us then cast off the works of darkness and put on the armor of light; let us conduct ourselves becomingly as in the day..." (Rom 13:11). Let us awaken from the trance that would have us preoccupied with what might happen or stuck in what has already happened. Let us awaken to the present moment in which we are alive and viable, real and empowered.

As we surrender moment by moment to life and what it brings, we decide how we will respond. When we respond according to what we believe instead of to what is happening, then we transcend circumstances and empower ourselves anew. Deciding how we will respond to what life hands us is, after all, the only real freedom we have.

In prayer and meditation we come to accept ourselves and our human condition. From this acceptance of what is comes the serenity we seek. Our anxiety calls us to grow from where we are to where we need to be. As we integrate what is with what can be, we come to know the peace of wholeness. "How true it is, Lord, that all our troubles come from not keeping our eyes fixed on you" (Teresa of Avila).

Sometimes it helps relieve our anxiety if we repeat a mantra that is especially meaningful to us. It may be a single word or it may consist of a phrase or two. The important thing is that it promote a sense of assurance within us. We may use such names as "Abba," or "Yahweh," or "I Am." We may want to remind ourselves that no matter what happens, "I'll handle it."

"All will be well," or "I breathe in love, I breathe out love," or any combination of words that promotes heart peace. There is something soothing and comforting about repetition. Eventually, the prayer on our lips and tongue becomes a prayer of the heart. The more we repeat it, or let it be repeated within us, the more we ground ourselves in the reality of God. Our mantra continually brings us into consciousness of the presence of God.

Sometimes prayers we have memorized can be very soothing to us in the midst of our anxiety. Letting our mind go to the words and letting the words go to our heart brings a healing peace. The following prayer by Spiritual Director Kathryn Kelley is both a desperate plea and a listening of the heart.

Heart Peace

I am waiting for you, Beloved of my soul,
and I find my aloneness frightening.
Let me know you are here with me in my agitation,
as I stumble and fall in my weakness.
Give me a sign to ease my fears and give me strength.

My precious love, my life.
Rest your trembling soul in this present moment.
Awaken, my love, awaken to where you are.
You are nestled safely in my tender heart.
Your innocence is cradled in my love.
You are my lover, you are my life.
You are my blood, as I am yours.
You are everything to me.
Nothing can separate us.
There is no aloneness.
We are all one-ness.
Stay awake, my love, stay awake.
Breathe my love, as I breathe yours.
Remember you are always and all ways in my heart.
Let the gentle pulsing of my heart comfort you.
Here there is only peace,
a peace passing all understanding.
Be with me, my love, be with me.

3

Healthy Anger

ANGER HAS A PURPOSE in our lives. Once we accept it as a natural, God-given emotion, we must then practice expressing it in ways that are not harmful to ourselves or others. Anger needs to be communicated to others, not used to intimidate or manipulate them. Anger equips us with energy to bring about necessary changes in our lives, but because of its awesome power, anger must be controlled. That is, it must be congruent with the circumstances and must not cause harm.

Wholeness does not require the rejection or suppression of our angry feelings, it requires that we courageously embrace all of who we are, including our angry selves, and allow the transformation that comes.

What Is Anger?

Anger is perhaps one of the most powerful emotions the human being can have, yet there is something even more powerful — the ability to harness anger and to use it for good.

What is anger? Anger is an emotional and physical energy that builds within us, it is a sign that something is not right, a message to us that we or our loved ones are being threatened in some way. Sometimes the threat is real and sometimes it is imagined, yet our anger does not know the difference and responds in any case.

Our anger energy can be allowed to flow or it can be stifled. But in either case, our anger will not go away until it has been dealt with.

Getting angry is as much a part of our humanity as getting sad or joyful. What is not necessarily basic to the human phenomenon is the manner in which we get angry. This we learn from our environment. It can help us to understand how we came to handle our anger the way we do.

Even from the beginning of our life we were constantly learning from our environment. As we grew through our first years of life we were attuned to the moods, feelings, and ways of being of those around us, especially those who took care of us.

As infants nothing was as important to us as survival and anger seemed like a threat to it. As infants we believed we needed to be lovable in order to survive. Anger meant someone was unhappy with us and would probably abandon us. Abandonment meant we would surely die, thus anger equaled death.

Family Influence

It is not easy for some of us to feel, much less express, our anger. For one thing, anger has long been an uninvited guest by society in general, and maybe our family in particular. As children, some of us were discouraged from feeling anything, including anger. As a result, some of us don't even know when we are angry.

Unfortunately, this is how our emotional system works. We can only shut down one emotion by shutting down all emotions, and shutting down the whole emotional system is tantamount to depression.

How was anger expressed as we were growing up? Was there a lot of yelling? Was there physical abuse? Did members of our family withdraw into a silent punishment of others? Was anger used to manipulate others or to cut them off or emotionally annihilate them? What was it we saw growing up. It is important to remember this because it probably has much to do with how we decided, albeit unconsciously, to deal with anger ourselves.

Maybe we were told as children that anger was so powerful that it could actually make our parents sick, or even kill them. Did we hear a parent say, "Don't make me angry, you know I have this heart condition." We may have become so afraid of what anger could do that we also became afraid to feel it, much less to express it to others.

We need to ask ourselves what were the verbal and nonverbal messages we heard about anger. Did getting angry mean we weren't loving or nice? Did getting angry mean the end of our peaceful image? Did it mean we would become alienated and lose the love of others? Did getting angry mean we would lose control?

As we remember how we came to learn our response to anger we can become more aware of the inappropriate and sometimes destructive ways in which we express our anger or react to the anger of others, and we can learn new, more constructive ways to deal with anger.

It is right to fear anger because, if misused or misdirected, it can be a weapon of destruction, but we can become so afraid of anger that our fear makes us prisoners of it. Either we are controlled by our own anger or we are shackled with fear of others being angry with us. In fact, we may have developed a hypersensitive awareness of others' anger, which can immobilize us or make us feel victimized.

A healthy relationship can withstand properly expressed anger, and, in fact, become healthier from it. On the other hand, even properly expressed anger threatens to destroy relationships which are based on a neurotic kind of love that demands only positive emotions and unquestioning devotion.

Suppressed or Misdirected Anger

We have come up with many ways of denying our anger. Some of us think we can deal with our anger like we would deal with a brushfire. All we have to do is hose it down with water and everything will be all right. We just take a cold shower or a drink. Some of us try to deal with our anger by distracting ourselves with television, shopping, eating, or some other form of addiction. But of course, the only way to deal with our anger, as with any of our emotions, is to deal with it.

Sometimes we try to rationalize away our anger. We don't want to feel anger toward another person because he may not be able to take it or because she doesn't know any better or can't help what she does. Some of us tell ourselves that only fools or out-of-control maniacs get angry.

Some of us squelch our anger with a controlled, monotone voice, others of us disguise our anger with sorrowful tears, anything to keep from showing our angry selves.

When we attempt to anesthetize ourselves to our anger, we automatically become numb to all of our emotions. In the transaction we lose our spontaneity, our sensitivity, and our creativity. We can become anxious and depressed as a result of suppressed anger. We may find ourselves overeating, not sleeping well, or turning to addictive practices in our attempt to relieve ourselves. These addictive behaviors may include abusing substances, and forming disastrous relationships.

Our unresolved anger may show up in our behavior in other ways. We may treat others with hostility. When we refuse to confront the true object of our anger, we are apt to transfer our anger to a safer target, like our wife or husband, friend or child. We may sabotage others or ourselves; we may be habitually late or forget important responsibilities; we may provoke others; we may fight against authority; we may act out sexually; we may become compulsive jokers or teasers; we may be bigoted; we may become destructive; or we may become hypochondriacs.

Our suppressed or inappropriately-expressed anger may affect our bodies adversely. Besides heart disease, other diseases such as cancer, high blood pressure, disturbed digestive systems, asthma, respiratory problems, and migraine headaches may result, as well as backaches, neckaches and sore muscles.

Sometimes it is easier for us to stay with our feeling of hurt than it is to feel our anger for having been hurt. Of course we need to feel and express our hurt, but when we stay in that emotion in order not to feel our anger, then we tend to get stuck in a victim role. Allowing our anger to be felt and expressed empowers us and helps us move from the victim role to a place from which we can better protect ourselves. The move from hurt to anger is obvious in our body language, also our voice stops whining and becomes strong.

Some of us will allow other, more acceptable emotions, to substitute for anger. If it was acceptable to be sad in our family, then even if we are actually angry, we will feel sad. If depression was preferred to anger, we will do depression even when we feel anger. Other, more "acceptable" feelings which we substitute for anger, may include sadness and levity.

Sometimes the opposite is true. We hide other feelings under our anger. If anger was the only feeling that was allowed to us growing up, it may be that we substitute it for our unresolved grief, sadness, hurt, or fear.

We think that by getting angry at ourselves instead of at someone else that person will not abandon us, but, in fact, we end up abandoning ourselves. It is true we need to avoid exploding our anger onto others, but we also need to avoid imploding our anger into ourselves. We need to know why we are so angry at ourselves, then we can allow our anger and let it be transformed into corrective action.

Sometimes the problem is not that we are not willing to be angry, but that we are not willing to let go of it. We may be holding on to our anger for a secondary gain. It could be the sense of power over the person we're angry at; it could be that the anger we feel allows us a sense of control (real or imagined); or it may be that anger gives us a reason to avoid communication and intimacy with others. We may stay with our anger because it helps us to feel safe and protected. We feel less vulnerable when we keep others at bay with our anger.

Sometimes we hold onto our anger in order to hold onto a relationship — even after the relationship has ended. Our anger can help us to avoid the feelings which may lie beneath our anger, such as sadness, grief, and fear.

Some of us prefer to remain in the role of victims. In fact, in some ways, our victimization may have become a part of our identity and we don't dare give it up lest we give up who we have become. Originally, we do not choose to be victims, but, ultimately, we choose whether or not to stay victims.

These, usually unconscious, secondary gains keep us stuck in our anger which, in turn, keeps us stuck in our life.

Healing Old Anger

On the other hand, the anger we feel today may be very much a part of our healing from past hurts. It may be that we are finally feeling the anger that we were never allowed to feel before. It may be that our anger is what enables us now to stand up for ourselves and for the part of us that was wounded before. Our anger may now be the energy behind our new-found assertiveness and our willingness to reclaim that which has been taken from us.

The important thing is to use our anger, if necessary, to set boundaries and regain our personal rights, but not to stay in the anger and become victims all over again.

Before we can deal effectively with our current anger, we need to deal with our old anger, that is, any anger that has been unresolved and just packed away in the basement of our psyche.

Sometimes the intensity of the anger we feel seems disproportionate to the circumstances which prompt it. This may be because the immediate circumstances are merely a trigger that taps the reservoir of anger which we have stored for a long time. If, for example, we harbor a lot of resentment deep in our unconscious for our mother for overly controlling us, then the slightest sign of control by anyone else prompts our anger.

Anger that is suppressed into our unconscious becomes dangerous because it goes unchecked and unmanaged. Suppressed anger does not want to stay suppressed and it works hard to surface one way or another. It may show up in unmanageable and destructive ways. We may not be in touch with our old anger, but we are in touch with the pain of ulcers or other physical ailments. Suppressed or distorted anger will manifest in hurtful words, sarcasm, or inappropriate teasing, unsolicited criticism, nagging, or blind rage. Suppressed anger may show up in a more covert manner as well — the silent treatment or with-drawal. Unconscious anger may show up in our hostile treatment of others and in self-hatred.

Part of the process of healing from our childhood wounds is to experience, acknowledge, and express all of our emotions, including our anger. Bringing our anger from the unconscious to the conscious level enables us to confront its sources and to make the necessary connections for better understanding. Once our anger is conscious we are in a better position to deal with it effectively.

Expressing Anger

Once we realize what our anger is all about we need to let it be expressed openly. Sometimes it is appropriate and productive to express our old anger directly to the person we are angry at. Sometimes direct expression is counter-productive, and it is better to write a letter which goes unmailed, or to talk to an empty chair, imagining that the person we're angry at is sitting in it listening to us.

Beating pillows as we express our anger may be very effective in cases of pent-up rage. It is not effective for the normal range of anger. The more aggressive anger therapy that entails beating pillows and the like is not an endorsement of violence. Rather, it is an acknowledgment that much of our anger and rage is stored in our tissues, muscles, and bones. Expressing our anger physically as well as mentally and emotion-

ally in a focused manner enables us to bring wholeness and completion to what may be scattered and
incomplete. This approach to working through our
old anger should be limited to cases of old, impacted
anger.

When we find ways that can express our unresolved
anger properly, we are able to finish it. When we complete our anger in an appropriate manner, our whole
emotional selves are opened up. As we stop suppress-
ing old anger, we also open up access to the rest of our
emotions, allowing healing of them as well. When, on
the other hand, we allow the non-directed expression
of our old, unresolved anger, it may get out of control
and hurt us or others.

We need to accept that our angry feelings are a normal and healthy part of our human emotion. We need
to deal with our anger as it comes up, not much later
when it has either lost its effect or has snowballed into
much more than was originally warranted. Sometimes
it does help to count to ten and get some perspective
before we express our anger, but it is important that
we not let it go too long.

It helps us to find out who we are angry at and then
to direct our anger toward that person rather than at
ourselves or at an innocent bystander. Sometimes we
are not angry at anyone in particular, but rather at the
situation with which we are faced. Putting words to
this anger makes it less vague.

As we dare to express our angry feelings toward
others, it is important that we let them know what

they have done or failed to do and how that has re-sulted in our anger. "You did so and so and I am angry with you." It is not an effective expression of our anger to blame, shame or insult another. In the expression of our anger we need to take responsibili-ty for it.

In many cases anger is met with rejection and dis-approval from others. For women the case is even worse. In our society it seems more acceptable for men to express anger than for women. When a woman gets angry she is discounted as irrational or even crazy. When a man is angry, he is more likely to be considered "assertive" or "forthright." But in gen-eral, men too are discouraged from expressing anger. Consequently, many of us are afraid to feel our anger.

When done appropriately, expressing our anger to those toward whom we're angry means that we care enough about ourselves and our relationship with them to tell them how we are being affected by them. It means that we want to see changes that will enhance our relationship. The expression of our anger is an investment in the relationship. But because expressing our anger openly to loved ones may mean to us that we will be abandoned by them, it takes great courage to do so. When we express our anger to others we take a great risk. It is helpful to us when our significant others are willing to let us feel and express our anger toward them without becoming defensive or leaving us physically or emotionally. It is helpful to them when we do the same.

In the expression of our anger it is not necessary to yell or in any other way intimidate the person we're angry with. At the same time, it is important that our expression, including the inflection and tone, of our words, be congruent with what we are feeling inside. To tell someone we are angry with them in a near whisper does not truly convey the level of our emotion. Strong words can be helpful when expressing strong anger. To deny our anger to someone who can see and hear that we are seething gives mixed messages and leads to confusion and mistrust in the relationship. To say to someone that we are angry with them, while at the same time smiling or even laughing or speaking meekly from our hurt, can be equally confusing.

Why should we express anger? Because by expressing it, it gives us a chance to look at it as a feeling, and to realize that we are separate from our feeling. We can have a feeling, like anger, yet we can return to our basic self, the part of us we sometimes call the "observer." It is a peaceful place from which we can watch our anger without judgment.

It is with the help of our expressed emotions, including our strong emotions such as love, hatred, grief, and anger, that we are moved through our wounds toward healing, and through dissolution toward wholeness.

Anger comes in all colors and sizes. When we are under the impression that anger can be expressed in only one speed — rage — then it is no wonder we avoid it whenever possible. But if we consider that our anger is like a keyboard of varying degrees of intensity which we can press according to the circumstances in which we find ourselves, then we may not be so afraid to be angry. Our intensity of anger is not the same, for example, when someone cuts us off in traffic as when someone burns down our house. Learning to express our anger appropriately necessitates learning to use this keyboard appropriately.

Prayer and Forgiveness

Prayer is important in dealing with our anger, but we cannot pray away our anger. Prayer and meditation is not a place to hide from our emotions. On the contrary, it is a place where we become more attuned to our emotions and gain insight into how to utilize our emotional energy.

Prayer enables us to open to our internal self where we hear the voice of God. But all the prayers in the world will not help us unless we also act in our external world. Our prayer will give us the courage to be real with our anger, even if it means a confrontation.

If our prayer is to be authentic, if it is to be true and open communication with God, then it must include our deepest and strongest emotions. As we pray, we need to let our anger out. Whether or not our anger is directed at God, it must be expressed. If our heart is angry, then in prayer, we give our anger to God along with our heart.

It is important that we don't use forgiveness to wipe away our anger, for this would be just another way to suppress or deny it. In the forgiveness process it is essential that our emotions, including anger, be experienced, acknowledged, and expressed before we forgive. Otherwise our anger will be merely covered over with our words of forgiveness.

Indignation

If we can shed the tears of God, we can also express God's anger. Our eyes see the suffering in the world, and the God within us cries. We witness life's atrocities, and the God within us becomes incensed.

There is a part of us that becomes indignant when we witness extreme injustice or cruelty or the gross mistreatment of God's creation. We become indignant at the starvation of millions in deprived parts of the world, while those with the power to alleviate their plight do nothing. We become indignant at the atrocities perpetrated against defenseless children by those who abuse them sexually, emotionally, physically, or otherwise. We become indignant at the senseless killing and mayhem of innocent people that results from political and cultural wars. We become indignant at those who violate our Earth in the name of progressive economics. We become indignant at those who usurp their authority and treat others with no respect for their human dignity.

The part of us that becomes indignant is the part of

us that really loves and cares. This is the part of us that cannot be oblivious to what happens around us. This is the part of us that feels on behalf of God.

Indignation is not vengeful. It does not mirror in action the cause of our indignation. Sometimes our indignation cannot act at all, but it can always be felt, it can always be expressed.

Our indignation is a cry from the depths of our soul that lets it be known that something is dreadfully wrong and will not be tolerated. It is a gesture, however powerless to change things, that must be made. It is the word that breaks the silence that perpetuates the injustice.

We believe anger and indignation to be ungodly, yet it is God whom we will find standing next to us, shaking a fist and screaming loudly that the injustice we witness must stop. God's indignation is felt and expressed through us, sometimes helplessly and in vain, yet always passionately directed against the inhumanity we witness.

We feel the pleasure of God because we love; we feel the sadness of God because we love; and we feel the anger of God because we love.

Transformation of Anger

Doing away with anger is not what is asked of us by life. What is asked of us by life is lovingkindness from which comes forgiveness and the effective expression of our anger.

The psalmist writes: "Be angry, but sin not; commune with your own hearts on your beds, and be silent" (Ps 4:5).

It is in this silence — in attentiveness to the present moment and the present emotion — that the transformation of our anger can take place. We need first of all to be aware of our anger. We need to treat it with respect. We need to accept it as a legitimate part of who we are. We need to stay with our anger for as long as it takes, watching with it, seeing what it is we need to do with it. As we dare to stay with our anger, we allow it to be transformed into constructive, life-giving energy.

What does it mean to transform our anger into constructive energy? First, it means that we must stop long enough to recognize it as a powerful energy that can be used for good or bad. Second, it means that we can choose to use it to communicate the problem before us to ourselves and to the one we're angry with. Third, it means that we use the anger energy to motivate us to take whatever action is necessary to bring about the necessary change. This means that we pass up the temptation to flee the situation and hide in our silence. Instead we choose to confront the situation and the person who is the object of our anger and to deal with the problem.

Through all this, we remain with our anger, we feel it, we experience it, we do not judge it, we merely acknowledge that it is a part of our present reality. We don't stifle the spirit of our anger, but neither do we just let it run rampant and uncontrolled.

We can use our anger as a powerful healing force to bring about change where change is needed. As we use our anger effectively, we continue to re-empower ourselves. The energy of our anger can be the fuel that propels us into action where fear may otherwise immobilize us. Our anger can serve as the catalyst that gets us unstuck from an undesirable situation.

As we sit with our breath coming in and out, we can allow our anger just to be without judging it as good or bad, desirable or undesirable. As we just sit with our anger and keep returning to our conscious breathing, we do not try to suppress our anger, we do not try to push it away, we do not try to talk ourselves out of it, we simply observe it and care for it with love as we would a child.

Sitting with our breath and our anger, we are allowing ourselves to enter into the anxiety of experiencing our anger and learning what we need to do next. As we dare to stay with our anger in the present moment, we also become aware that our anger is a part of us, but only a part. We are not our anger. There is so much more to us than our anger.

Everything depends on how we perceive our anger and how we choose to respond to it. Our anger can be the block that keeps us from living fully, or it can be the energy that propels us toward a healthy relationship with ourselves, with others, and with life.

The Anger In My Heart

Bless, dear God, the anger in my heart.
May the spirit of my ire give me courage to confront.
May the energy of my indignation move my hand
against injustice.
May the power of my rage be harnessed
for the good of all.
Let the love that fills me in the quiet hour dispel
my wrath, my rancor, my animosity.
Give words to my resentment that it too may dissipate.
Bless, dear God, the anger in my heart.

4

Depression's Promise

HOW CAN THE AGONY OF DEPRESSION *be connected to a spiritual path? The spirit, after all, is life-giving, while depression stifles and kills. But this is precisely how depression throws us into the depths of our spirituality. The shadow that overtakes us is so dark and heavy that it binds us to purpose and leaves us buried under the rocks of fear and anxiety. Here, at the place of hopelessness and despair, we are forced to question all that we have taken for granted. We are thrown back onto ourselves and our own resources. We are challenged to carve out a faith from little or nothing.*

In the midst of the darkness, our eyes are opened to that which really matters. The depression which levels all that we have known, also calls us to a higher plane.

The Agony of Depression

Depression is hell. In our depression we feel so worthless. We are self-accusatory and self-critical, and we assume everybody else feels the same way about us. Mentally, we feel incompetent, and emotionally, we are dead. We have no will power and no sense of self-control. We don't know what we want, and we are indecisive about everything, even the most simple thing. In our depression we feel frozen, immobilized. All is black and ugly, and the demons of our unconscious come out of the cellar to haunt us.

Depression is hell because hell means separation, "to be fenced off," and in our depression we are separated not only from the rest of the world, but even from ourselves. We are left in this pit of anguish, devoid of our vitality. Our zest for life has been stolen, our grasp on life has been broken. We are totally devastated in spirit.

Our depression goes beyond sadness. It is a sense of mental woundedness that only seems to get worse and worse. We are filled with apprehension and anxiety, and we experience a skewed reality filled with delusions and paranoia. We suffer from a paralysis of the will, and our only belief is in our helplessness. In depression we lose all meaning in life. There is nothing for which to live. We have lost our life force.

In depression nothing matters. We just don't care one way or another. This is the nature of depression: flat, unemotional, apathetic, gray, purposeless, and dreadful. When we enter into depression we lose whatever hold we have on our emotional attachments. The descent into depression is a descent into the cold, dry world of our masculine energy. We leave behind the feminine energy that keeps us involved in life. We are left with no feeling, no faith, no love. We are left in spiritual poverty.

The Roots of Depression

Our depression may be the result of chemical imbalance, what psychiatrists call endogenous depression. Sometimes our depression is genetically passed on. This depression that emanates from within responds well to medication. But depression can also be our way of coping with the wounds of our soul. In this case, healing comes through a combination of medication and therapy.

Depression can be our way of avoiding the memories of traumatic events. As long as we stay depressed, we don't have to allow the thoughts and feelings that accompany certain events into our lives. Dealing with the trauma of our lives must be done carefully. Lifting the depression abruptly without dealing with the trauma may leave us defenseless. The therapy must include the establishment of new and healthier lines of defense as we uncover the trauma.

It may be that depression is signaling to us that we are in an unworkable situation. This may be about our marriage, our work, other relationships, or other circumstances. Whatever the case, our soul may be pleading with us to change things because they are no longer tolerable. Sometimes our need to withdraw from the world is overwhelming to us, and the only way we will allow ourselves to do it is through depression. Depression gives us permission to go to that quiet place. When we learn to stop and rest as a regular part of our living, then we will not need to enter depression in order to rest.

Depression may also be the result of unresolved grief. Perhaps we have lost a loved one through death and have not completed the grieving process. Maybe we have lost our job through attrition or retirement and our major role along with it. Sometimes a major change, like a move from one city to another, has not been assimilated psychologically, resulting in depression. The end of a relationship, for whatever reason, needs to be grieved. Getting older and facing physical changes and illnesses can also cause a grief that, unresolved, turns into depression.

Depression should be avoided whenever possible. Once depression has come, however, we not only need to treat it, we also need to learn from it the lesson it wants to teach us. We need to let it take us where it must. It is important that we not remain in our depression longer than necessary. We need to stay there only as long as it takes for us to hear its message and to allow its purpose to be realized within us.

It is not enough to medicate depression, however.

We need to delve into its causes, especially if the depression has been chronic. Even a low-grade depression that has persisted most of our lives must be seen as an indication that there is a wound within us that needs healing. Sometimes the origin of depression is so deeply buried in our unconscious that it takes a lot of therapeutic work and much patience to tap it.

The Message of Depression

In depression we are forced to learn humility. That is, we come to acknowledge our strengths and weaknesses, our assets and liabilities, our potentialities and our limitations. Strangely enough, in the midst of our depression we discover an endurance which we have not known before. We lose everything and are forced to fall back on our most basic selves. It is here that we begin to use our core resources.

Maybe we have suppressed our rage lest we become violent or lose control. The result may be depression. Maybe we have been profoundly hurt in the past, but have not allowed our hurt and sadness to surface. The result may be depression. It is as if our soul declares, "If you don't let me feel this one feeling fully, I will feel nothing at all."

When we are depressed we are allowing the dark, negative part of ourselves to manifest. Perhaps we have hidden these parts from ourselves in the past.

Now depression carries them to the surface and allows them the attention they have needed. It is all right to be dark, negative, down, and empty; not just light, positive, up, and full. Depression allows us to embrace those parts of us which we would rather lock away in a cave.

Could it be that we need to enter into that dark mood of depression periodically in order to incubate new life? Depression can be a time of transition for us, a time of becoming who we need to be. The depression experience can be excruciating, yet, having moved through it to the other side, we may be left stronger, wiser, and more alive than ever before. The more we fight the depression that comes the more it overpowers us. Instead, we need to cooperate with our depression. We need to see it as an opportunity to heal what we cannot heal in any other way. When we give our depression respect and attention, we allow ourselves to learn from it what we must learn.

Spirituality has to do with deep connections with our soul, that is, with the part of us that transcends our ordinary, day-to-day identities. When we step out long enough from our frantic lifestyles, when we really look at ourselves and allow our true selves to surface, we may have no choice but to enter into depression. Perhaps this is why we stay so busy, trying to outrun the darkness, operating with the delusion that if we just keep moving, depression will not over-take us.

It is in depression that we can see things as they really are. From this baseline we are able to remember things from our past that we had forgotten or repressed. We are able to revisit past losses and truly grieve them, in some cases for the first time. Sometimes we discover that we have been sad much of our lives, but have not known exactly why.

Through the valley of the shadow of death we enter into hopelessness, then, gradually, we move toward hope, toward a belief against the evidence. Then we embrace a God who is bigger than the one we knew before.

In the midst of depression interesting things are happening within us. There is a constant breaking down of our false selves and a building up of our true selves; there is an expulsion of the superfluous in our lives and an inclusion of that which is essential for healthful living; there is a dying to old ways, and a resurrecting into new life.

Depression seems like lost time, yet, it is a time of fecundity. It is during depression that we are forced to face those persons and life events which have hurt and disappointed us greatly. During depression we allow ourselves to face the failures of our past. As we heal from our depression we learn new ways to live in order that we don't repeat what has been harmful to us.

Depression is a trial of the soul. We have within us all that it takes to heal from our woundedness, and our depression is a part of what it takes. First, we must enter into the darkness for there is where we will see the glimmering light of hope.

The Loneliness of Depression

Depression is a lonely place to be. Inside we are crying out to others, "My heart is nearly broken with sorrow. Remain here and stay awake with me" (Mt 26:38). We want so much to receive compassion, comfort, and companionship, yet, outwardly, we don't even know how to ask for what we need. Even though we are surrounded by others in the midst of our depression, there is a point beyond which no one can accompany us, not even through empathy. There, we must pack for one and continue the journey by ourselves. Others have seen us through grave moments of our lives, but the moment of our greatest passion is a moment alone. Now we must bear the pain without the support of others, without their strength, without their presence. Now, in the midst of our fear and anguish, we reach out and there is no one there.

Our depression can bring out the worst in others. It triggers for them their sense of helplessness and reminds them of the dark places in their own heart.

It is at this time of existential loneliness that we feel abandoned, empty, vulnerable to the wolves. There is no place else to turn but within to the secret place of the soul. When we let go of our reliance on the things of the world to protect us, when we release even our loved ones as saviors, we come to discover the one and only source of our security; we come to know God who will never leave us alone because we are a part of God.

Our basic human loneliness, which cannot be allayed even by those who love us most, is the condition that turns us back to God. It is a thirst that can be quenched only at the fountain of God. We must exonerate those whom we have expected to alleviate the pain of our depression, for they cannot. Theirs is but to walk with us to the door of our soul. From there we must enter alone, believing, "You will leave me all alone. Yet I am not alone, for my Father is with me" (Jn 16:32).

The Salve of Love

Sometimes all we need in our depression is a kind word, a healing touch, a gesture of concern, a moment of patience. Because depression lingers, it is important that the action of love be constant. The daily phone call or post card from a friend or relative can make all the difference in the world to us when we are depressed. The willingness to just sit and be with us in our depression is the best medicine of all. It is amazing what love can do, even in the face of an apparently hopeless depression.

Love melts the ice of depression because it was the

lack of love that wounded us in the first place. Gestures of love, that is, kindness, acceptance, gentleness, nurturance, and respect, make up the salve that heals our wounds. Where once there was neglect, there now can be attention; where once there was abuse, there now can be tenderness; where once there was detachment, there now can be involvement. These are the things for which our soul has hungered. This is what we needed then and this is what we need now.

Love encourages us to risk life again. With the encouragement of others we can begin to venture out of our protective cocoon, we can begin to explore the offer of a new world. Love provides an environment in which we can move at our own pace, without pressure to get well. Love offers a place to be ourselves, no matter how broken we may be. Such love may come from family, friends, or professional helpers. Such love is inspired by God. Such love is the bounty of the fortunate.

Loved by God and loved by those around us, we allow self love. It is now that winter turns to spring. Within us is a love that lifts us from the depths and heals our wounded soul. It is the love that completes us.

God Is Forever Coming

God is forever coming because God is the creator of life.
God is coming because God is the
light of understanding.
God comes to us because God is love, and
love cannot help but share itself with the beloved.
It will be a long and lonely winter,
and we will pray, believing in the seed that is planted
in the depths of our soul.
We will wait and watch,
expecting the promise of new life
filled with the joy of God's eternal presence.

5

Transforming Grief

❦

LIFE IS CHANGE, *and with change comes the pain of letting go of what has been and adapting to a new reality. The pain of letting go is what we call grief. Because change is constant in life, grief is constant also. As we lose what we have had, we enter into a place for wounded souls, a place in which we can wail and groan from the agony of our loss. It is a place in which we realize the full nature of our love. The poet Khalil Gibran wrote that, "Love knows not its depth 'til the hour of separation." It is in this special place that we are reminded of our own mortality, and our existential anxiety of being separated from life. It is also in this darkened place that we begin to change ourselves. There is death within us, and there is also the seed of new life.*

Adapting to the Loss

There is no set time schedule for the grief process. Each case is different. The length of time that it takes to heal from the loss of a loved one through death depends on the type of relationship we had with the deceased, the role they played in our life, the type of death they experienced, the degree of trauma we experienced with the death, our previous experience with loss and grief, and a myriad of other factors. Usually, the grief journey takes from one to two years, but may take more time in cases of sudden and unexpected death or death by violence, such as suicide or murder.

We talk about healing from our loss, but the healing is not the healing of a disease. Grief is not an illness. We heal from the wound which our loss has inflicted on us. We are not sick in our bereavement, but we have been dealt quite a blow. As we heal we accept that our loved one will not return to us physically. We adapt to our life as it is now, after the death, and we change our perspective of life in whatever way necessary to accommodate our new world. This may mean that we set aside expectations we once held; it may include changes in our behavior; it may even affect how we perceive ourselves.

Our grief has plunged us into an emotional depth we did not know existed within us. If not for our loss, we would never have known this profound pain. To have run the gauntlet of emotions, including shock, pain, depression, fear, loneliness, meaninglessness, emptiness, guilt, and isolation, and not to succumb, leaves us strong and capable enough to take on almost anything that life hands us. We will not be consoled, but we are comforted. That is, we are given the strength to cope and to make it through the night of sorrow. Paradoxically, the pain of the death makes us come alive. We discover that the power to heal lies within the wound itself.

Our healing does not lift us above our feelings, but, in fact, allows us to enter into them more completely. On the other side of grief there is abundant living and this includes the fullness of our emotions. Before our loss and grief we may have blocked or ignored our affective selves, now we are open and attentive to what we feel.

As we face our loss and move through our bereavement we learn that we cannot take anything for granted any longer. In the final analysis, we are alone in our grief. Others offer their invaluable support and we are grateful for it, yet, we come to realize that we can no longer depend on anyone else to make us okay. It is up to us alone to handle what is before us. We alone must take responsibility for our life from now on, and to give it meaning and purpose.

When we can ponder the life and death of our loved one without inordinate emotional reaction, and when we can remember our loved one without the intense psychic pain we experienced in the beginning, we are well on our way to healing.

Along the journey of grief we must first recognize the loss that has befallen us. We must acknowledge the death, then react to the separation, experiencing and expressing all the emotions that come. Then we must identify all the secondary losses that stem from the death of our loved one, and remember and re-experience all that we have had together. We must remember the good as well as the bad. Then we must begin to relinquish our attachment to our loved one. We must let go of many of the assumptions we had about life, and we must adjust to a new world, a world that no longer includes our loved one. As we allow a new relationship to develop with our loved one, we also allow ourselves to change. Then, and only then, do we begin the process of reinvestment.

Internalizing Our Loved One

We have lost so much. We will never see our loved one again. We will not be a part of the future of our loved one nor will our loved one be a part of ours. We miss our loved one's embrace, smile, idiosyncrasies, phone calls, friendship, and way of being. We have lost someone we love, and yet, there is a way in which we have not lost our loved one at all. In a way that knows no bounds of time or space or physicality, we are even closer to our loved one than before. We cannot be more intimate than when we are connected at the soul.

It is by internalizing our loved one that we can truly

heal. Our healing comes, not by forgetting our loss, but by integrating it into the fabric of our life. Our healing comes, not by separating ourselves from our loved one, but by internalizing our loved one, and letting our loved one become a part of who we are now. Our loved one has died, yet lives on within us. By internalizing our loved one we release what was and take into ourselves the essence of what is and will forever be.

We become one with our loved one. Death has separated us and we suffer the agony of hell. But our love is stronger than death. As we take into ourselves the transcendent being of our loved one, we enter into the union of souls. Where we have been broken and anxious in the wake of our loss, we become one in the peace of heaven, a union eternally unbroken.

Although we are not the embodiment of our loved one, we can allow ourselves to identify in some ways with our loved one. We are ourselves, but we can, if we choose, take on some of the aspects of our loved one's life. We can emulate some of our loved one's characteristics that we admired and respected. We can realize some of our loved one's dreams, and we can complete some of our loved one's plans.

As we walk in the world in which our loved one no longer walks, we can find creative ways to commemorate the life and death of our loved one. We can do things and support projects that were dear to our loved one in life. We cannot live the life of our loved one, but we can honor it through our own life.

It is not necessary for us to sever all connections with our loved one. The death has ended a life, but it has not ended the relationship between us and our loved one. We need to develop and nurture a relationship with our loved one even in death. This can be healthy and life-giving. Of course, we release the physical and concrete, but we embrace that which transcends life as we know it. It is a spiritual connection that can never be severed.

Some of us believe that if we allow the emotional energy which we have invested in our loved one to return to us, that we are being disrespectful to them or in some way are abandoning them. But this is not so. We take back our emotional energy and reinvest it in other life-giving relationships, including a new and different relationship with our loved one. What we are releasing is the relationship as it existed before our loved one died. Through our grief and through our healing, we join with our loved one at a higher plane.

The integration that takes place as we heal includes not only the life of our loved one, but the death. Who we are now and who we are becoming includes all that has happened to us. We need not become professional mourners, but we need to incorporate into our life the reality of the death that has touched us.

A New Perspective

Perhaps our basic personality remains the same, but after the death of our loved one we change in so many ways. We no longer see things as before. Our view of life is altered dramatically because now we see it in contrast to death. Our view of death is different than before, if for no other reason than that it appears more imminent. Some of what was so important to us before is not so important now, and what didn't seem to matter before, now matters greatly to us. In some ways we are more patient, and in other ways we find we have little or no patience. The nonsensical, super-fluous, and superficial annoy us greatly. Life is more real to us now and we insist on everything in it being more real.

We have had our world turned upside down by the death of our loved one, and everything we have believed in is thrown into question. Our trust in life, God, and ourselves has plummeted, and we are not sure about anything. Ironically, it is this lost state of mind that moves us to a deeper faith because we must cling to something that we cannot see, hear, or feel. We are forced to consider new and different possibili-ties and this propels us into a newfound freedom of choice. This is not to say that we have chosen our loss, rather, that our loss has opened up alternatives which we would never have considered before. We can do things we thought were beyond us. We are better able to endure suffering and accept disappointments. We have survived a tragedy and this has revealed to us an inner strength we did not know was there.

We need to allow grief to come and we need to allow grief to go. Sometimes we cling to grief as if it were the last vestige of the relationship we share with our loved one. When even a glimpse of joy comes our way while in the midst of our sorrow, we need to trust it and appreciate it. These moments of respite, though few and far between, are a gift. Let us accept them graciously and use them in our healing.

We will always feel some sadness, but it will be a different kind of sadness, a sweet pain in our heart, and not a wrenching agony in our gut. We may shed tears from time to time, but they will be tears of gentle remembrance. In our healing we begin to accept our loss mindfully and emotionally. Soon we are able to be in a world that is different because it holds a new reality, a reality that does not include our loved one as before. Little by little we assume control of our life again. We allow ourselves to change internally and externally to become congruent with our new reality. This includes letting go of the roles we used to play with our loved one that no longer apply. At first we learn to live without our loved one. Eventually, however, our healing takes us to a point in which we are learning to live more independently with ourselves.

Although grief is a part of love, grieving forever is not a sign of a deeper love. Loss of a loved one interrupts our life, to be sure, but a permanent interruption is not indicative of a permanent love. On the contrary, love is life-giving, love allows freedom, love begets actions. Our love for one who has died is best manifested in how we go on living our life. Of course we pine and yearn for our loved one, of course we hurt tremendously for the loss, and are deeply saddened by the absence. But our love would have us be appreciative of the time we shared with our loved one, and in love we remember with fondness all that was. In love we honor the life and death of our loved one as part of us dies and returns to life. Slowly, but surely, we move through our grief to the other side. Our love for ourselves and for the one who has died opens us to the gift of healing.

We may be afraid to reinvest in relationships. We fear that we will only suffer the excruciating pain of separation again. Some of us decide never to love again, lest we suffer yet another loss. But, even the pain of another loss would not be as great as the pain of emptiness and meaninglessness that comes to a life without love. Yet, even after we have adjusted socially to our loss and have begun to reinvest in life again, this does not mean that we have returned to who we were before the death of our loved one, for we will never be the same person again.

Our healing is enhanced when we assign meaning and purpose to the life and death of our loved one. As we give meaning and purpose to the death of our loved one, we also give meaning and purpose to our own life. Where once there was just an empty darkness, we move toward a fulfilling enlightenment. We dedicate our life to our loved one. The death has left us empty, yet we live our life more fully in the name of our loved one. In our grief we hate life, yet through our grief we come to cherish it.

A major part of our healing has to do with forgiveness. We come to the point where we can and do forgive our loved one for dying, and for hurting us in any way. We also forgive our loved one for leaving us behind to struggle with the living. We move from forgiving our loved one to forgiving ourselves for any harm we may have caused. We also forgive ourselves for surviving. As we forgive, we release our hold on guilt, shame, and anger.

Our choice is this: we can endure the grief process and merely make the best of a bad situation, or we can allow our grief and its impact on us to lead us to a deeper and more meaningful life.

From our darkened room of grief we begin to venture out. Little by little, we step into the light. It is difficult to emerge. We have become accustomed to the safety of our cocoon and we are afraid of life. The more we come out the more we realize that we must choose life.

Transformation

We have been so opened, so exposed by our grief, that it is inevitable that issues old and buried come to the surface to demand attention and closure. With help we can take advantage of this opportunity and work through past grievances and heal old wounds. Through the experience of our loss we are compelled to face some of our issues of abandonment. This leads to healing on a broader scale. And as we deal with our abandonment issues in the wake of our loss, we learn

to care for ourselves emotionally. We also prepare ourselves to face future losses without the same overwhelming fear of abandonment.

In the beginning of our grieving process we are
physically a mess. It doesn't matter much to us what
happens to our body. We don't care if we die along
with our loved one so we don't really want to take care
of ourselves. We sleep poorly, our appetite is gone,
and we are fatigued and vulnerable to illness. As we
heal, we regain our vitality and begin to take responsibility for what happens to us. We tend to ourselves
with better nutrition, exercise, and rest. We regain the
control over our body that we had lost. As we begin to
heal we experience increased energy, we sleep better,
and we are less vulnerable to illness. Instead of being
anxious we become more calm, and in the place of our
constant sadness, a more positive attitude develops.
As our energy returns and our depression lifts, we may
be ready to take on a new job, begin a new project, get
more education or training, do volunteer work or
other activities that bring us fulfillment as never
before.

Even when we are well into our healing, we remember. Perhaps our pain is not excruciating, and maybe
our tears are not as profuse, but we still feel a sadness
in our heart, a pining in our gut, and a missing in our
mind. The memories that come are a gift. They connect us to what once was and will never be again.
They are pieces of our life as we shared it with our
loved one. When the memories come let us honor
them, savor them, cherish them, and let them soothe

our wounded heart. Some of the memories are unpleasant, and we need to remember them as well. One indication of our healing is when we can look back at the life of our loved one with a more realistic eye, acknowledging the good and the bad, the joy and the pain of their time with us. Our remembrance must be real if it is to be healing.

There are special times of remembering: anniversaries, certain events, seasons of the year or holidays, during which our grief returns. These are not setbacks, but merely our grief still working itself through. Healing does not mean forgetting. There is a difference between forgetting our loved one and not dwelling on our loved one all the time. We are able to remember fondly, yet, our mind need not be obsessed with the memories.

In the beginning it is torture for us to remember our loved one because we also have to remember that our loved one is dead. As time passes and healing takes place, we can remember our loved one without the intense pain, and we can even laugh and be grateful for the time we did have together. We may be tempted to stay in our regret of lost opportunities and years unlived, yet, we can choose instead to celebrate all that our loved one was in our life and is in our heart. We lament what has been lost, then we thank heaven for what is gained.

Perhaps the most difficult part of our bereavement is saying good-bye to what has been. It is hard to stop yearning and longing to be with our loved one. But it is because we say good-bye to what we love that it becomes a part of our memory, and more, it becomes a part of who we are. The paradox is that by letting go of what we love, it is ours to have forever more. It seems that the integration of our total life comes about only when we have allowed the disintegration of its parts.

Our loved one has died and a part of us has also died. Through our grief process we experience a death and resurrection. As part of us dies, new life emanates from us. We become more understanding of the pain of others, and we are more compassionate toward suffering in the world. There is a new strength that begins to emerge from our fallen self.

In our healing we move from our old way of doing things to a more self-loving way. No longer do we live only for others. Now it is our personal fulfillment which we seek. Now we are important, too. As we reach out in life, as we dare to risk, our trust begins to mend: trust in ourselves, trust in God, trust in others, and trust in life.

Hope begins to make its entry into our life in subtle ways. We may begin making plans for the future, we may find ourselves reaching out to others in their need, or we may even risk loving again. Yes, our trust begins to return as we dare to risk living and loving again. It is not a belief that we will not be hurt again, but a knowing that whatever comes our way, we will handle it. We know because we've done it. We gain self-confidence and are willing to try new things. We enter into activities which bring forth our proficiency and our talents.

We know we are healing when our creativity begins to make itself known to us and others. From the ashes of the Phoenix comes new life in the form of our creativity. Regardless of the medium, our creativity is our inner life manifesting itself, signaling the coming of spring after a long, cold winter. In our bereavement our sense of self has been crushed. Our creativity helps restore our sense of self because what we create is a part of who we are becoming.

Grief, when does it end? Perhaps our grief is never truly completed, but we can eventually recover an important degree of our stability, our energy, and our hope. We come to a place in our mourning where we can begin to enjoy life again, and even invest ourselves in it. We can be healed and still be grieving. We are left scarred by the loss of our loved one, but our scar only means that our wound has been healed.

Healing Our Soul

If nothing else, our grief opens us wide open. Never before have we been so vulnerable. It is at this shattered place in our life that the spirit of God enters. In our woundedness we are open to the healing of our soul, in our brokenness we are open to the possibility of our wholeness, and in our confusion we enter into faith. We find that if we are to communicate with our loved one, we must enter into our spiritual selves. Thus, the death of a body brings the resurrection of our spirit.

In our newfound spirituality we see death differently. No longer is it an end of life, but a transcendence. Our sense of God becomes larger and our purpose for living takes on new meaning. But even our spirituality cannot save us from what must come — the devastation, the desolation, the drama of death played out. The message of hope must not be used as a quick fix. We cannot circumvent Good Friday to get to Easter Sunday. Our sorrow will turn to joy and our darkness into light, but we will not flourish again until we have first been pruned back to our basic self. Perhaps it is our wounded spirit which is the last to heal. For so long during our grieving we have been unable to really pray, but the nature of our prayer does not matter as much as that we pray. Our prayer may consist of nothing more than a sigh of letting go or a silence of deliverance. God knows our pain because God knows our love. God hears our prayer because God is within. God is with us in the wound and in the healing. If we hold God accountable for the death of our loved one we can't exactly turn to God for comfort or support. When we realize, however, that God does not cause bad things to happen to us or to our loved ones, but is with us constantly as we struggle through our sorrow, then we can begin to let the love of God into our life. It comforts us to know that, although God cannot reverse the death of our loved one, God is with us in our grief. It empowers us to know that God gives us everything we need to get through our terrible ordeal. It brings us peace to know that God is life and God is death, and that neither we nor our loved one will ever be beyond the touch of God.

In the Face of Death

Even in the face of death you call us
to experience our life in the fullest
and to respond to it with the passion that is ours.
You would have us confront the loss
and let the pain have its way with us.
You descend with us into a sorrow so deep
that it seems joy is lost to us forever.
You are with us in our anger, you feel our helplessness,
and sense our fear of abandonment.

Through our loss and grief we come to realize that a
part of us has died and a new part has been born.
Now there is new energy
that propels us into higher living.
Only you, dear God, who mourn with us,
can lead us back to love; only you,
who die with us, can lead us back to life.

6

Beyond Loneliness

❦

FACING OUR LONELINESS is very hard to do. It is one thing to enter into our solitude by choice, there to discover the mysteries of our inner self. It is another to be excluded from life itself, and to be left feeling abandoned and unloved. We welcome solitude because it is nourishing to the soul. It is a reflection of the connectedness we have felt before. Loneliness is frightening to us because it triggers scenarios from our past in which we have been left behind, ignored, unattended. Our fear of loneliness is fear of being separated, of not belonging, of not mattering, not feeling life. It is the cause of our existential anxiety.

From loneliness, as from all of our emotional states, we can learn and grow. We can move through loneliness to wholeness or we can remain stuck in our loneliness. It is our choice. As we allow ourselves to experience our loneliness and to learn of its source, we regain the lost connectedness and we discover an inner reality from which we can never be separated.

The Pain of Loneliness

Loneliness can be a cornerstone of our self-actualization, or it can be the boulder that crushes our life. Each one of us decides what to do with our loneliness, and our response to it becomes a way of life.

The feeling of loneliness is sometimes confused with other emotions. For example, although loneliness may result in depression, it is not the same. While we may seek solitude for the peace and re-creation of the soul, loneliness is an emotional isolation in which we become painfully aware that something is missing in our life. Loneliness can be excruciating. It is a state in which we are more conscious of what we don't have than of what we do. In loneliness we feel loveless, and nobody can live without love. What is especially dreadful about loneliness is the belief that we don't matter to anyone. It follows, then, that neither do we matter to ourselves. Or perhaps it is because we don't matter to ourselves that we feel we don't matter to others. Either way, it becomes a painful cycle. Loneliness hurts so much because it includes the sense of being abandoned, and, ultimately, of annihilation.

Many of us deny ever experiencing loneliness. We are afraid to look vulnerable and weak. We admit to being "alone," but not lonely. Yet, our loneliness is an inherent part of the human condition. It is a natural process of life that touches us all. Our very self-awareness predisposes us to loneliness. Even as we become conscious of our separation from our mother at birth, our loneliness begins. Perhaps it doesn't end until we enter unity through death.

It is our fear of loneliness that immobilizes us more than loneliness itself. Perhaps at the basis of the fear of loneliness is our fear of death. Death is the ultimate separation, it is what is beneath all of our fears. Our fear of death begins in our infancy and continues throughout our life.

Living is Lonely

Not all loneliness is necessary or inevitable. Sometimes we create our own loneliness by the way we live our lives. It follows that when we purposely isolate ourselves from others socially, emotionally, physically, or spiritually, we will experience the sense of separation. Usually, however, loneliness is imposed by circumstances and is not a matter of choice.

One adolescent may experience isolation when he is feeling ugly, unimportant, and unloved. Another may feel lonely when she is compelled to take a stand against peer pressure. One woman may feel lonely when she realizes that her whole life has been lived to please others at the expense of her own growth and welfare. Another may face loneliness as she leads a large organization or movement. One man may be lonely as he gives constantly of his time, energy and emotional self in a care-giving profession, yet receives little care-giving himself. Another may feel lonely as he struggles through a crisis alone. The journey of aging is lonely, as is the first day of school.

We experience loneliness when we feel misunderstood. We feel lonely when we enter into creativeness because it is something unique to us. We even feel loneliness when we are in love because, in our endeavor to become one with our beloved, we come to the stark realization that no matter how close we get to one another, we are still two separate beings.

Those who have been gifted with the ability to obtain an extremely high degree of knowledge or who have developed a higher level of wisdom sometimes find themselves very alone in the world. This is also true of those who reach positions of great leadership or who come to a spiritual enlightenment beyond that experienced by their peers. Those who are different from the norm also suffer from extreme loneliness. This may include those who have physical defects which distinguish them from others, or those whose sexual orientation differs from the majority of society. It may include anyone who marches to a different drum. It seems that the more unusual a person is, the more lonely he or she is going to be.

Our loneliness may be triggered by a myriad of events or situations, even by the weather. Special days, such as Christmas, are painfully lonely to some of us because they remind us just how lonely we really are. But these are just the triggers of a deeper source of loneliness. It helps to get to the root of our loneliness and to understand the reasons behind it.

Roots of Loneliness

We are lonely now because we were lonely a long time ago. If as an infant we experience the presence of our mother, and are able to internalize the sense of her presence, we come to feel secure even in her absence. With the internalized presence we are able to be alone without fearing annihilation. This is the foundation on which we build our sense of secure solitude. Without this internalization of our caregiving mother in the early stages of our life, we are bound to suffer from much loneliness later. As we grow older we continue to make our "being" contingent on the presence of others, and when they leave us we fear we will surely die.

The loneliness that comes in certain situations in our adult life is aggravated by the experience of loneliness that is triggered from our early childhood. Our pain is compounded by our past experience and our reaction to it may be out of proportion. Only when we return to the point of our original wound and deal with it will we be able to experience the loneliness that is part of normal living without undue reaction.

Some of us have been so hurt by others at an early age that we have set up all kinds of defense mechanisms to protect ourselves from further harm. This has set us apart from others and has condemned us to a state of isolation and unrecognized loneliness. We have lived our lives separated from others and have not known just how lonely we really were until someone touched us with love. Then we came to know how deadened we were in our aloneness. The new relationship may have introduced us to a whole new world of friendship, but, at the same time, it made us vulnerable to the pain of loneliness that comes with being alive.

Some of us have been raised in an atmosphere that was repressive and controlling, leaving us at a social and psychological disadvantage. Not having been allowed to develop our own sense of self, it became difficult for us as adults to have healthy relationships with others. We may desire closeness with others, but we don't know how to express these desires. This may have resulted in a life of chronic loneliness.

Some of us have been more inner-directed than others most of our lives. This has led to shyness, avoidance behavior, and a general sense of not belonging. Our nature is often misunderstood, ridiculed, and sometimes persecuted. In a world where the outgoing, ebullient personality is admired and preferred, the more quiet, reserved person knows loneliness well.

Escape from Loneliness

Sometimes the pain of loneliness feels more severe than physical pain. The psychic pain is so great that we beg ourselves to anesthetize it. We turn to alcohol and other drugs, we overeat, we get overly busy, we become involved in intense relationships, we work harder and longer, we embark on adventures and take risks, all in an attempt to medicate away the pain we feel in loneliness. Such relief does not last long. We may be numbed out for a while but then the pain returns and we end up with even less hope of any alleviation.

We evade, deny, and otherwise escape the experience of being lonely. Unfortunately, our attempts to avoid loneliness only produce more loneliness. In our fear of loneliness we separate ourselves from others. Our illusion is that others are responsible for our loneliness, but as we flee, we run right into what we dread the most.

Friendship, the source of nourishment that we need so desperately, comes as a result of our reaching out toward others. It requires active and affirmative participation in life. But the alleviation of loneliness is not just a matter of us being more pleasant or outgoing. It doesn't have to do with us meeting people or getting more involved in activities. Yet, this is the advice we receive from others. We want nothing more than to let go of our loneliness. We hate it and sometimes we hate ourselves for allowing it to overwhelm us so. No matter how hard we try to change ourselves and our circumstances, our loneliness remains.

We are so desperate to overcome the pain of loneliness that we are sometimes tempted to give up our individuality and submit to a relationship of total dependence. A part of us reasons that it is better to be in an unhealthy relationship than to be lonely. When we feel incomplete and empty, we sometimes believe that others can complete us and fill us up with life. Of course, this is impossible and our futile attempts to be made whole from the outside only leave us frustrated. The loss of our individuality results in the greatest loneliness of all. If even after we have connected with a significant other, we are still lonely, then it is a terrible loneliness indeed because then, even our expectation of being rescued from our loneliness by another is shattered along with our hope.

Being with others does not by itself alleviate the sense of loneliness. We can be lonely in the midst of a crowd or we can experience no loneliness even when we are alone. Others can be there for us even in the most excruciating events of our life, but ultimately, we are alone as we experience them. As we go through grief after the loss of a loved one, as we create from our depth, as we confront a serious illness, as we suffer the effects of a natural disaster or the trauma of a violent act against us, or as we enter into death, we must do so by ourselves. Granted, the pain of our loneliness is eased when we have the support of others' presence, but the experience is ours alone.

Serial relationships have to do with our quest for that which will erase the emptiness from our heart. It is a chase that will end in vain because what we desire so desperately cannot be gotten from without. Our loneliness is not about others, it is about ourselves. Until the separation is healed within, no relationship will meet our needs.

Sometimes we act as if the last thing we want is

involvement with others. We cover our loneliness with a mask of hostility or apathy toward love, pretending that we don't want it anyway. We go to great lengths to protect our undeveloped ego.

The more we attempt to escape our loneliness, the deeper our loneliness wounds us. We yearn to be with others, yet, we are frightened by the possibility. We are anxious about our loneliness, and, at the same time, we are enraged because we have been excluded from the whole. The struggle is fierce, but it is internal.

The Face of Loneliness

We don't like to see others in a state of loneliness because it makes us very uncomfortable. We don't want them to suffer pain of any kind, including loneliness, yet, there is more to it than that. We also don't want to get in touch with our own loneliness through them. Therefore, we quickly try to "help" the lonely person to a better place. We may introduce him to others, we may invite her to be with us, we may advise him to get out more, or we may recommend to her that she change in order that others will be attracted to her. We will offer anything except what the lonely person needs most from us — acceptance. In order to alleviate our own discomfort we end up rejecting the lonely person's feelings. The most loving thing we can do for the lonely person is to accept him or her along with the pain of loneliness that is experienced. This acceptance will do more for the lonely person than any other anti-loneliness measures. We must make peace with our own loneliness if we are to accept the loneliness of others. Otherwise, we merely contribute to their loneliness.

This does not mean that we are helpless in our response to the loneliness of others. In fact, our loneliness calls us out of ourselves toward a more compassionate awareness of others. It helps us to hear the lonely cries of others and to respond to them. We are compelled by love to act on behalf of those who suffer from the kind of loneliness that kills. There are those who are imprisoned in bodies wracked with physical pain, those who live out their moments in nursing homes, hospitals, and prisons. There are those who are homeless and poor, and there are those who are emotionally broken. Here we need to do more than accept their loneliness, we need to help them in their circumstances in whatever way we can.

Search for Intimacy

We try so hard to end the behavior that points to our loneliness, but our behavior is only symptomatic. Nothing will change for us until we are willing to address the nature of our aloneness.

Most of what we do is motivated by our deep desire to rid ourselves of loneliness. We don't want to be alienated. We want to end our separation. We want more than surface living. We desperately need to touch and be touched at a deeper level, at the level of true friendship, at the level of the soul. Loneliness is not alleviated just by being with somebody, it has to be a certain somebody with whom we connect intimately. The attachment we seek is one of closeness and meaningfulness. It is at this level that we receive the nectar of life. As human beings we yearn for the intimacy that is part of being connected at the soul with everyone who has ever lived. All of us in some way are striving for communion with everything around us: nature, persons, God, life.

The lonely person knows that life is not supposed to be this way. The lonely person remembers at a deeper level the wholeness that has been shattered, the cord that has been broken. Loneliness is no more than the pining for the lost oneness, the sacred togetherness that once was.

Beyond Loneliness
to Wholeness

How do we defend ourselves against the onslaught of loneliness in our lives? We draw from that which is our essence, our innermost self. It is from this part of us that has existed since before we were born, that we tap the energy and the force that can move us beyond the pain of loneliness. It is to our soul that we can cling when we feel abandoned even by God. As we return to ourselves we return to God, as we return to God we are sent out to touch the lives of others, as we touch the lives of others, we are also touched. This is the compassionate circle of love.

Our loneliness exposes us to our incompleteness and moves us toward wholeness. Through the experience of loneliness we are brought more deeply in touch with the true nature of our existence. Possibilities are revealed to us that we have not known before. But we cannot explore those possibilities unless we are first willing to experience the pain that accompanies the loneliness.

Our loneliness enables us to understand that we are indeed separate from others. At the same time, it lets us know that we need others involved in our life in profound and significant ways.

We heal our original wound by tapping the unconditional love of God and loving ourselves with it. We give to ourselves the attention and the importance which we needed from the beginning. We make the connection with ourselves that was not made with our caregivers, and we return to a constant presence with God and with ourselves. We release our hold on that which keeps us at the periphery of life. We allow ourselves to enter fully into life, including our loneliness. This does not require that we stop being afraid, it only requires that we be afraid and do it anyway. In other words, it requires that we tap the courage which we find at the core of who we are. Only by courageously facing the inevitable loneliness that comes can we convert it to new and fruitful life. Facing our loneliness openly and living with it honestly, we develop our inner resources. By allowing ourselves to experience, not the fear of loneliness, but loneliness itself, we come to learn true compassion, to risk intimate relationships, and to grow emotionally and spiritually.

Our spirituality cannot save us from loneliness. Having faith in the unconditional love and constant presence of God does not by itself mitigate our loneliness. On the contrary, our spiritual development exposes us even more to our naked humanity and all that comes with it, including the pain of loneliness. While our faith does not rescue us from loneliness, it does help us to experience it fully and to transform it into personal growth and life-giving creativity.

Through the faithful act of surrender into our loneliness, we may be able to transform it into solitude, which is the fountain of life itself. Reaching inward we touch our existential loneliness which is an intrinsic condition of our humanity. Our soul yearns for an eternal communion which can only be consummated with God. Only by our willingness to endure loneliness will we be allowed to enter into the depths of our own being. To reject our loneliness is to remain on the outside of ourselves forever. There are those who have come to know themselves like never before while on a solo expedition or an extended solitary confinement. They experienced the loneliness, to be sure, and they also experienced a flight into innerspace.

In the midst of our painful loneliness we are compelled to consider what is important to us and what is not. From this point of agony the meaning of life is questioned and our purpose for existing is reconsidered. The question is: what meaning will we give to our loneliness? The choice is ours. We can allow the loneliness that comes with life to shrivel our soul, or we can experience it fully as it moves us into unity of all souls. As we confront the alienation of loneliness, we pass through deep darkness and melt into a bond with all of God's creation.

The Hour of Loneliness

The loneliness comes over me like a cloud. God, I feel abandoned, even by myself. The skies are dark and my heart is empty. All around me is desolation. Will no one hear me? Will no one understand?

In my loneliness I travel far away. No one knows me there, no one really cares. I feel unloved, insignificant, and all alone. My connection with life itself is broken, as is my heart. I want to die. I want to end the pain.

In my delusion, I chase elusive butterflies. I look to the external for some relief, but there is no reprieve. I am separated from all that really matters.

From the midst of my nothingness, I hear your still, small voice. It calls to me in supplication: "Stay with me in the hour of loneliness." I dare to stay, allowing what will be.

In the hour of loneliness, I tell you of my pain, I cry the tears of a newborn child, pining for its Source, yearning for its Destiny. You speak to my soul: "Can a mother forget her infant, be without tenderness for the child of her womb? Even should she forget you, I will never forget you" (Is 49:15).

I believe you, God, even in my disbelief. I surrender to you, God, even in my fear. I am one with you, God, even in my separation. You are the foundation of my life, the ground of my being. Everything else is added to that.

It is not my life, but yours, that returns into the world. The loneliness that once divided me from others, now connects me with their pain. Because you understand me,

I understand myself and others. Because I am important to you, I am important to myself and others are important to me. Because you love me, I love myself and others.

In the hour of loneliness, I am not alone, for you are with me always. My pain remains, but is transformed into compassion for a lonely world. My tears still fall, but it is joy that brings them forth. The barren desert in my heart is changed into a place of springs, a fountain of your love.

In the hour of loneliness, I am one with you and with all of your creation.

7

Freedom through Forgiveness

FORGIVENESS IS A WAY OF LIFE. It is the cradle into which we are born, unconditionally open to who we are, not holding against us who we are not. It is the ultimate acceptance of what is before us without judgment, and without the imposition of expectations. The spirit of forgiveness is the basic nature of a loving God who stays with us even when we stray a far distance, a God who does not judge, but only waits for our return.

As the spirit of forgiveness moves through our world it touches those of us who feel separated from one another, from ourselves, from God, and from life. It is the hand of an alienated friend that invites us to reconnect, it is the canceled debt, the burden set aside, the second chance. It is the voice of God bidding us to come home where we belong.

The forgiving heart holds nothing back, least of all love. It dismantles the machinery of war and finds the common way. To forgive is to begin anew, it is beginning fresh every moment. The old dies off even as it happens and we are left with the purity of a newborn babe. Holding nothing against ourselves, nothing against any other being, nothing against life, we are at the same time the forgiver and the forgiven. To forgive is to believe in the ever-changing, ever-transforming, ever-redeeming nature of eternal life.

Forgiven by God

Before we can free ourselves from the debt we owe to life, we must first be willing to let God absolve us through forgiveness. Think of it! No matter what it is that we have done or failed to do, in the wake of our repentance comes our absolution.

But some of us believe in a God who holds our wrongdoing against us and who loves us less because of it. Some of us believe in a God who rewards those who get everything right and punishes those who don't. Some of us believe in a God who only forgives those who are worthy of being forgiven. Some of us believe that God cannot possibly forgive us because what we hold against ourselves is so awful, so unpardonable

But worthiness has nothing to do with forgiveness, it comes to us through grace, simply for the asking. God does not just love us, God loves us unconditionally. The forgiveness which comes from that unconditional love is also unconditional.

We have been taught that we are unworthy because of our original sin. God would have us embrace our original innocence. We have been told that as human beings we fall short of the glory of God, and that only by some sort of sacrifice can we be redeemed. God would have us know that we are the glory of God, and that it is not sacrifice that is required, but mercy.

Often when we realize we have strayed off course we condemn and banish ourselves from the presence of God. The more we move away from God, the more capable we are of living against the will of God. It becomes a vicious cycle that can only be broken by our willingness to accept the forgiveness of God, regardless of how far away we have wandered.

It matters that we recognize what we have done and that we confess it to the God within. Forgiveness comes from mercy. Mercy taps the generosity of God. We are forgiven by God even as we dare to ask forgiveness, and we are made whole again.

To believe that we are forgiven by God even before we trespass is not a license to live irresponsibly. We must remember that we are each capable of horrendous crimes against God and all creation. Only by staying in the constant presence of God and letting God live through us can we know the will of God and do it. Our willingness to see the error of our ways and to make the return is the real transforming miracle for which heaven rejoices.

Coming to believe that we are completely forgiven by God, that is, that nothing is held against us, can be a transforming moment for us. When we truly believe that God cleans our slate and encourages us to begin anew, we are overwhelmed with the awesomeness of such love.

The state of the forgiven is a state from which we live and love. No longer do we dwell on our misdeeds, no more do we carry the burden of our faults. To be forgiven means that we know that, although God holds us accountable, nothing is held against us. We, in turn, hold ourselves accountable, but hold nothing against us. As the forgiven, we hold others accountable for their action and inaction, but we hold nothing against them. To "hold nothing against" means that we are free to deal with whatever is before us without being bogged down with inordinate anger, resentment, and hatred, or with a nagging need for revenge.

We cannot receive God's forgiveness deep in our heart without being compelled to forgive from the same depths. Forgiven by God we are moved to forgive ourselves and those who have trespassed against us. Forgiveness begets love and love begets forgiveness. The forgiveness of God is constant, we are the only variable.

Forgiven by Others

No one who has ever been forgiven can deny the life-giving impact of that forgiveness. Forgiveness from another can be the key that opens the door to our heart. To repent and be forgiven by the one whom we have sorely injured is to be exposed to a power beyond ourselves that gives new life amidst the ashes of death. We come to realize that only love has the power to move someone to forgive, and only forgiveness has the power to transform.

It seems that the greater the wrongdoing for which we are forgiven, the more grateful and loving we become. As it turns out, those of us who have been granted the greatest mercy are the ones who now feel the most loved. Knowing love like this enables us to love others in like manner.

Repentance and forgiveness act together as a catalyst that changes us forever. We are no longer stuck in our indebtedness to another. We are now ready to live differently so that we may bring good, not harm, to others. Being forgiven does not take away our guilt, it does not alter what is. We must still suffer the consequences of our action or inaction. Being forgiven changes nothing on the outside and everything on the inside. Our gratitude for this second chance prompts us to change from within. In gratitude we re-set our direction and map out a new course — to live now with the understanding that we need the help of God lest we fall back into our old, injurious ways.

Expressing our repentance and seeking atonement is important, but it is not enough. We must follow up with changes that ensure we will not repeat our offense.

When we confess, whether it be to a friend, a family member, a counselor, a priest, or to a support group, we do several things that help restore our sense of wholeness. First, we own up to our wrongdoing and take full responsibility for it. When we do this we empower ourselves to avoid repeating our mistake. Second, our expression of contrition for what we have done recognizes the debt that is owed to others and asks forgiveness for that debt.

When we ask forgiveness from others it is not

enough to feel guilt or sorrow for what we have done. Asking to be forgiven must carry with it a desire to make amends. The injured person must be utmost in our mind as we ask forgiveness, not just our own well being. Perhaps we can never really restore things to their original condition, but we can offer to repair what we can and to compensate for what we cannot.

If we want to be forgiven by those whom we have hurt we need to ask for their forgiveness. While there is no guarantee that the forgiveness will be offered, it helps our odds if we ask for it. Sometimes it is best to say, "I'm sorry that I hurt you. Please forgive me." Other times it suffices to apologize with a simple, "I'm sorry." In true repentance we can ask forgiveness, but we need not make excuses for ourselves or give justifications for what we have done. No reservations or qualifications are necessary. We simply acknowledge our misdeed and ask forgiveness.

The granting of forgiveness is a gift, but so is asking for it. It helps those whom we have hurt to know, first, that we are confirming that they have been hurt; second, that we were responsible for the hurt; and, third, that we regret having offended them.

When we have been forgiven we are not the only ones to benefit from the forgiveness. Surely those who forgive us are set free from what they hold against us, but beyond that, those who are indebted to us will also benefit from our forgiveness of them. As we are forgiven we are inspired to also forgive. Forgiveness is contagious, and its impact is far-reaching. God only knows the extent to which one single decision to forgive affects others down through the ages.

In the end, it is of no use to plead forgiveness from those whom we have hurt if we are not prepared to accept that forgiveness. We prepare by forgiving ourselves.

Forgiving Ourselves

Even though we are forgiven by God or others, our spiritual solvency will not be restored until we also forgive ourselves. Yet, forgiving ourselves is one of the hardest tasks we face. We tend to be so much more judgmental and severe with our own wrongdoing than we are with that of others.

Self-forgiveness is not just a matter of saying to ourselves, "I forgive me." It requires sinking into the innermost room of our being and standing there naked before our intimate God. It requires recognizing the error of our ways and expressing our sorrow to that God whom we cannot fool with false emotion or empty promises of reform. There, at the base of our existence, we come face to face with the God who refuses our indebtedness. As we come to accept God's forgiveness, we learn to forgive ourselves.

Some of us refuse to forgive ourselves because we believe that in doing so we abrogate our responsibility. This is not so. Self-forgiveness does not cancel out our responsibility, it is a decision to not hold against ourselves the errors we have committed. We must still hold ourselves accountable, we must still face the consequences of what we have done, and we must still work to change ourselves in such a way that we are not apt to repeat our mistakes.

Some of us refuse to forgive ourselves because we feel so badly for what we have done and we believe we deserve to feel this way, but self-forgiveness does not take away our conscience. Self-forgiveness says to us, "You did wrong. Repent, make amends if you can, learn what there is to learn, and then get on with it. What will you carve out of today?"

To forgive ourselves does not mean that we are not guilty of the wrong we did. It means that, guilty or not, we no longer hold it against ourselves. We must acknowledge our action, take responsibility for it, and learn from it, yet, not let it separate us from ourselves.

Self-forgiveness is an admission that we certainly are capable of tremendous blunders that hurt others. It is an acceptance of our imperfection and an embracing of our total selves. To forgive ourselves is an act of humility.

Through self-love we come to self-forgiveness. We come to forgive our body for being too tall/short, too heavy/thin, too dark/light, overly endowed/under endowed. We forgive our body for being weak, vulnerable, lazy, sick, and for aging without our permission. We forgive our body for the pain it makes us feel, the tiredness it brings, and all its limitations. We forgive our body for its sexual nature and for giving us drives and urges which seem to take us beyond ourselves. We forgive our body for being in the dying process from the time we acquire it, and we forgive our body for eventually dying on us.

Through self-love we come to self-forgiveness. We forgive our soul for wandering off into the far country away from our source and destiny. We forgive our soul for being caught in the passions of life. We forgive our soul for forgetting what is real and what is bogus. We forgive our soul for living from fear instead of love. We forgive our soul for being seduced by the lure of the lesser treasures. We forgive our soul for insisting on its freedom and refusing to be harnessed. We forgive our soul for not forgiving.

As we forgive ourselves we enter into the valley of our shadows, accepting what is, developing what can be, always refusing to hold against ourselves what God has already forgiven.

Forgiving Others

Forgiveness is the art of letting go. It is an ability inherent in the human soul to heal itself; a power that frees us from the trap of victimization, and allows us to live without the encumbrance of a rancorous heart.

But forgiveness is not easy. It is a process that can begin immediately, but which takes time to complete. Sometimes we are moved to forgive prematurely, that is, our intellect tells us to forgive before the rest of us is ready to do so. We may believe that to forgive is the "right thing to do" and induce it from ourselves, but this is usually not effective. Forgiving because we should is like loving because we should, it is not authentic. There is a time for everything, including forgiveness. We need only to be open and ready to pass on the forgiveness that emanates from deep within ourselves. It is the energy of God.

Through forgiveness we allow our hurts to be transformed into lessons and opportunities for growth, we confront the brokenness in our lives and the alienation in our relationships, and we allow healing and reconciliation to take place.

Some years ago my son was killed crossing a street at the crosswalk by a driver who was not paying attention to the road. I remember that my forgiveness of the driver did not come quickly or easily. Oh sure, I told him I forgave him even as my son lay dying in the hospital, but this was only my intellect speaking. Deep inside I still had not really forgiven.

If the ability to forgive is seen as a virtue for which to aspire, we may be tempted to lay claim to that virtue by merely verbalizing our forgiveness, as I did initially. If forgiveness is understood as a process through which healing can take place, we may discover that we are not so ready to forgive.

The decision to forgive is not forgiveness. We also must decide to pass through the painful process of letting go. The process includes not only dealing with those who have harmed us, but also dealing with our wounds and our emotions about what has happened to us.

Until my whole self dealt with what had happened to me, until I identified my profound hurt and anger, until I allowed myself to experience fully these feelings instead of denying them or resisting them, until I took the time and effort to express these emotions verbally and nonverbally, I was unable to really forgive my brother from my heart.

We should not expect ourselves to forgive before we are ready. Forgiveness comes forth from us only after we have dealt with the impact of our injury and the ensuing emotions. Willingness is crucial for true forgiveness, and willingness cannot be forced.

Forgiveness takes time, we cannot rush it. It comes when it is ready to come and not before. It must move at its own pace and take all the time it needs to be completed. It is important that we not forgive before we have dealt fully with the injury done to us. In cases of severe and traumatic injury, for example, we need to come to a full understanding of our victimization before we can begin to forgive. The trauma must first be acknowledged and worked through. Forgiveness must not be used as an attempt to escape the feelings that arise from the abuse.

In order to forgive we have to have something to forgive, but if we are not in touch with what has happened to us and how it has affected us, we cannot let it go. In our low self-esteem, we may be unaware that we have actually been hurt by others, especially if we don't believe we are worthy of decent treatment. If we are unaware of being injured we cannot deal with the effects of the injury, and we cannot truly forgive.

Sometimes we are too quick to forgive, other times we are reluctant. We may fear that our forgiveness will be misinterpreted to mean that we are willing to be hurt again, or that we condone what was done to us. But it is important to remember that the action against us is not excused, it is forgiven. It is not a debt owed to us any longer, but the forgiven will still be held accountable for any future actions. When we forgive we set boundaries to protect ourselves from further harm.

Because we forgive others it does not mean that we do not act on our own behalf. It may be that our offenders have to be reported and even jailed in order to protect ourselves and our society from further harm. Such protective action is not inconsistent with forgiveness. Retaliation, revenge, and punishment, on the other hand, are.

When we forgive we do not excuse; we do not condone; we do not sanction. When we forgive we do not first come to "an understanding" of why those who harmed us did what they did. That understanding may come later. First, the hurt, the hate, the wanting to retaliate, all of these feelings must have their day in court. Forgiveness must come from a heart that is open and willing to confront the truth. We cannot dull our senses and lose touch with our feelings and call this forgiveness. As we release our feelings through forgiveness we can then begin to put things into perspective and try to understand. Forgiveness does not need understanding or perspective to happen. It does not have to be purchased with reason before it is offered. Forgiveness stands alone and it is free.

We may not want to forgive out of fear that we will have to befriend the forgiven or that we may have to like them. This is not so. When we forgive others it does not require that we befriend them, and it is very possible to forgive others whom we dislike intensely. Forgiveness does not obligate us in any way to the forgiven. Forgiveness has no prerequisite except the willingness to let the spirit of God move through us.

We don't have to trust those whom we have forgiven either. Forgiveness is not a declaration of trust. Neither is it an automatic return to the ways things were. If that happens at all, it may take time. When we forgive offenses by others we restore our soul and theirs, but we do not necessarily restore the relationship to what it was.

It is possible, however, that our forgiveness of others may clear away enough blockage to allow us to like them and even to become friends. After all, our attitude toward the forgiven inevitably changes with forgiveness.

We may be reluctant to forgive because we fear the loss of power or control over those who injured us. It is true, once we forgive we let go of any real or imagined power we may have. In forgiveness we recognize our equality with those whom we have forgiven. But, in fact, through forgiveness we gain back the power and control over our own lives which we had lost.

Our refusal to forgive, for whatever reason, keeps us in the role of victim. We may feel as though we are one-up on those who harmed us by keeping something against them, but in reality we are one-down. Forgiveness lets us be equal and releases us from the ties of victimization.

Forgiveness that is used to manipulate or control other persons cannot be considered forgiveness. Forgiveness has no conditions. It is pure gift on the part of the forgiver. The forgiven have not earned our forgiveness nor do they deserve it, and yet, we can forgive them. The forgiven may continue in their misbehavior toward us and, although we hold them accountable, we may also forgive them. In fact, those whom we are forgiving don't even have to know about our forgiveness to be forgiven. It doesn't matter whether they accept our forgiveness or not, it is still valid. It doesn't matter if those we forgive don't change their behavior; our forgiveness still frees us to move ahead. Forgiveness changes the heart of the forgiver even if it does not change the forgiven.

Sometimes it isn't an injury directly perpetrated by others which we have to forgive, but their failure to meet our expectations of them. Forgiveness helps us to set aside our judgment of them and to allow for the less-than-perfect human condition.

Social, cultural, religious, and personal differences abound in our world. Sometimes these differences get in our way. People believe differently then we do and live in ways we would not live. For this we forgive them. We do not have to adopt their ways or abandon ours, we only have to stop holding against them who they are and what they are about.

Forgiveness may seem impossible to us sometimes. There are offenses for which forgiveness seems out of the question, yet, there is no offense that cannot be forgiven, no matter how unforgivable it may seem. There is within us a spirit that transcends the impossible. There is within us the courage to let go and the faith to go on living. Forgiveness is prompted by our will, but it requires the help and the energy of the God spirit within.

We are unable to mark the beginning and ending of forgiveness. Old feelings may return much later when we remember hurtful times. This does not mean we haven't forgiven, it only means we haven't forgotten.

Forgiving is not forgetting. It is important for us to remember all that has happened to us in order to learn from our experience and to protect ourselves in the future. But although we may remember how we were hurt and by whom, once we forgive from our heart we are no longer broken by those memories. The memory of what happened to us becomes a part of who we have become, yet, after forgiveness we are no longer held hostage by the memory.

Even after we have forgiven others for hurting us we may still show signs of our woundedness. We may wonder whether or not we have really forgiven when we are still sensitive and not yet ready to trust again.

But although forgiveness begins the healing process, healing takes time. Through forgiveness we are able to remove the splinter from our side and cast it away forever. But we need to allow time and care to heal and close the wound.

Forgiveness is radical. Not only does it enable us to release what we hold against others, but it moves us to plead their case before the court of heaven. It compels us to identify with those who trespass against us, and to advocate on their behalf.

As we release others from what we hold against them, we also release ourselves from what shackles us to them. Forgiveness begets forgiveness and mercy spreads like wildfire. We have it in our power to let the spirit of forgiveness take over the world or we can block it right where we stand. We are the gateway through which the mercy of God flows into the lives of others.

The Way of Forgiveness

God of mercy, God of love, you live within my Self. To know your presence is to know forgiveness, to know forgiveness is to know the nature of your love.

Gone are the ties that bind me to my lesser self, open are the possibilities of new life. You forgive my failure to love, and love comes forth. You release me from my debt, and I give more than what I owed.

God of freedom, God of grace, you hold nothing against me, and I can do no less. Set free from the shackles of my sin, I also free others from their boundness to me.

The harm that is done cannot be changed, and I honor the reality of that which is. I may bleed and I may suffer and be left with less, yet, all that I hold against another I have the power to revoke.

God of peace, God of compassion, you touch the world through me. I am the voice of your amnesty, the sign of your forbearance. There is no mountain that cannot be leveled, no valley that cannot be filled.

God of redemption, God of life, I am forever innocent in your eyes; always you accept me, unconditionally you absolve me; your love compels me to forgive even as I have been forgiven.

8

Awakening Hope

❦

IT IS ONE THING TO HOPE in health, happiness, and good life, quite another to hope in all that comes with life, including suffering and death. This is not to say that we are to desire suffering and death, but rather, that even in suffering and death we dare to hope because, even there, we experience the presence of God. Regardless of the conditions or the circumstances of our life, if we believe God is with us, hope springs eternal. There is no place where God is not. The psalmist prays: "Where shall I go from your Spirit? Or where shall I flee from your presence? If I ascend to heaven, you are there! If I make my bed in Sheol, you are there! If I take the wings of the morning and dwell in the uttermost parts of the sea, even there your hand shall lead me, and your right hand shall hold me. If I say, 'Let only darkness cover me, and the light about me be night,' even the darkness is not dark to you, the night is bright as the day; for darkness is as light with you" (Ps 139:7).

Our hope, then, transcends what is before us, not by thinking about tomorrow, but by daring to stay in the present and finding God's love in the eternal now.

The Power of Hope

Hope is that spiritual power that comes from deep within our soul where God abides. It becomes the energy that moves us through the day, loving in the face of a loveless world. With hope at our core we can live through whatever pain and disappointment may come our way, and in the light of hope we can transform the tragedy and suffering which we find in the world.

Our hope is that no matter what occurs in our life, no matter what happens to us, there is a part of us that cannot be violated, subdued, or killed. Our hope is in that pure and holy part, that invulnerable, indestructible vestige of life — the soul, the center of our being. It is our soul that emits that life-force we call spirit. It is our soul that carries the energy of God into the world.

The dictionary defines "hope" as, "...the feeling that what is wanted can be had or that events will turn out well." But hope is more than wishing for or expecting something we want. It is more than believing something good will happen or expecting that everything will turn out for the best. Hope is more than not giving up, more than clinging to a dream. Hope is a deep knowing that there is more to life than meets the eye. It is a letting go of everything, then returning to embrace it with the arms of God. The good news of hope is that when we can touch our most sincere hope, we also touch the hope of God.

Scripture says, "We know that in everything God works for good with those who love him, who are called according to his purpose" (Rom 8:28). This does not mean that everything works out well for those who love and serve God and not for those who don't. Rather, the promise is that those who love God above all and who make God the center of their lives, find in that love and focus a way to make the best of the worst. Hope must be found in the darkness of the valley as well as the light of the mountaintop. Evil is as real as goodness, and both are part of life. We cannot wait to stamp out evil before we can be hopeful, our hope must come even in the face of evil. When our only hope is in the reality of God, we find God's meaning and purpose in all that happens. When our hope is in God alone, we are God's hope.

In hope we become true to our humanity. It is from here that we unleash the love force of God. Where we have been stuck, we are freed to move ahead; where we have been impotent, we become the power of love.

We may hope for all kinds of things: health, a new job, a good marriage, peace on Earth, etc., but as long we remain stuck hoping for what we want, we are unable to hope for that which is the most important to us. It is natural to hope for good things to happen to us and to those whom we love. In fact, it is important that we come to know what we want and don't want in life. Eventually, however, we need to expand the picture of life to include, not only what we know to be, but also that of which we are not yet conscious. As we move beyond our hope we move toward something even more significant than ourselves or that which we desire. We move to something beyond ourselves.

Hoping Against Hope

Abraham was 100 years old, yet he was told he would become the father of many nations. Hoping against hope, Abraham believed. What is it to "hope against hope?" Is it as simple as hoping for something that seems impossible? No, for this can sometimes be foolishness, not hope. Rather, "hoping against hope" means that even though we are naturally inclined to hope for certain things in life, there is an even greater hope deep within us to which we must listen. This internal hope is often different than the external hope. The internal hopes against the external. It is through self-abandonment that our true hope is found. Jesus assured his disciples that "...unless the grain of wheat falls to the earth and dies, it remains just a grain of wheat. But if it dies, it produces much fruit." He said that: "The man who loves his life loses it, while the man who hates his life in this world preserves it to life eternal" (Jn 12:24).

When we lose our hope, when we have no purpose in life, when we have nothing left for which to live, we enter into desperation. This is the door to a deeper life, a life in which we discover our most authentic hope. When we stop hoping, it is not an abandonment of hope, but a true entry into hope. We find that from the death of hope (hopelessness) comes the resurrection of the spirit (hopefulness). It is when we come to the edge of our limitations, when we run out of runway, when of ourselves we can expect nothing, that we dare to hope. In our inadequacy, our hope turns to the supreme adequacy of God; in our littleness, we defer to the incomprehensible enormity of God; and in our hopelessness, we enter into the holy hope of God. We pray as the psalmist did: "For you are my hope, O Lord; my trust, O God, from my youth, from my mother's womb you are my strength; constant has been my hope in you" (Ps 71:5).

Despair

Sometimes we have to be stripped of our external selves in order to become conscious of our internal selves. Sometimes we have to lose in order to gain. Carl Jung wrote that we find out what it is that supports us only when we can no longer support ourselves. Jesus also spoke of this: "Whoever would save his life will lose it, but whoever loses his life for my sake will find it." It happens like this. We come to a place of emptiness. We feel as though we are in a cave with no exits, no light, no air. We call out for help but there is no answer, there is no light, there is no hope. We despair. In our desperation we go even further into the cave, deeper and deeper into the abyss of hopelessness. We stop believing in our own ability to rise from this pit of despair. We stop believing in the power of others to help us. We even stop believing in God as rescuer, as protector, as overseer. We have nothing left. We are dead, or so it seems. From this apparent death comes the seed of life, life as we have never known it. This is not a life of resurgent energy and it is not filled with high emotion. It is not a life of glorious fruitfulness. It does not enter as a lion. It is just life, life as it has always been, is, and always will be. It is life that is authentic, even if not grandiose. The life that rises from the ashes is not as magnificent as the Phoenix, but is just as real. It is simple; it is small; it is slow. It is a life that emanates from the deepest caverns of our soul. It could not have come had we not plunged into the depths to liberate it.

The greatest of our powers is that we can commune with God; this is also our greatest hope. But even before we can enter the heaven of our communion with God, we must walk through the hell of our separation from God. In life we experience the abandonment and we experience the oneness. We echo the dying words of Jesus: "My God, My God, why have you abandoned me?" and "Into your hands I commend my spirit." Our hope is not a flight from despair but a confrontation with it, trusting in our ability to transcend it. The pain and suffering that are a part of life do not disappear by hoping, but in our hope they take on purpose and meaning and the power to transform us.

Our Truest Hope

In this life we are not sure of much, but our hope is completely confident in God. We may not always understand the power of God; we may not always recognize God's presence; yet, in the final analysis, we hope that the omnipotence, the omnipresence, the omnibenevolence, and omniscience of God prevails against all else.

There is a difference between hoping and holding onto our expectations. Our true hope opens us up to the movement of God; expectation imposes our will onto life. When we choose to hope, we let go of those expectations that bind us to a lesser life. When first we hope we assume incompletion, we want more than we already have, or we want to keep what we have without the risk of losing it. In hopelessness we expect nothing, and we cannot lose something we don't have. Through hopelessness we move to a new hope, a hope in the completeness of God, a hope in the wholeness of our soul.

When we allow ourselves to hope our truest hope, we allow the fears and insecurities of tomorrow to fall away from us. When we hope with our soul we place ourselves at the disposal of life and love, confronting what comes with the best of our ability and leaving the rest to God. This does not mean that we abdicate our responsibility for our lives, but, rather, that we respond to life with the hope of God. Jesus asked his followers to "Stop worrying. The unbelievers of this world are always running after these things. Your Father knows that you need such things. Seek out instead his kingdom over you, and the rest will follow in turn" (Lk 12:22).

With our hope in God, not much else matters. In hope we are able to set aside that which is superfluous, that which we may have outgrown, that which impedes our communion with God, and that which is less than authentic. But hoping in God does not mean that God is our last chance to get what we want, no matter what that is. It means that our desire becomes God's desire; our will becomes God's will. Our hope is in God's purpose because that is paramount to us. Even as we work to do God's will or to carry out God's plan as we understand it, our hope is in the power of God to help us do it.

Our truest hope believes not only in the glory of spring, but also in the bareness of winter. We believe that "The light shines on in darkness, a darkness that does not overcome it" (Jn 1:1). Our truest hope is found in the resurrection of life as well as in the journey into death. This is the hope of hope, that regardless of what is, it is in that reality that we find God. When we are truly hopeful we find:

> Success in the midst of failure
> Victory in the midst of defeat
> Joy in the midst of sorrow
> Generosity in the midst of greed
> Humility in the midst of pride

Uniqueness in the midst of the ordinary
Courage in the midst of fear
Healing in the midst of pain
Reconciliation in the midst of anger
Faith in the midst of doubt
Peace in the midst of conflict
Good in the midst of evil
Wholeness in the midst of brokenness
Light in the midst of darkness
Love in the midst of apathy
Hope in the midst of hopelessness

The Greatest Treasure

Our prayer of hope is not one in which we beg God for that for which we hope. Our prayer of hope is to quiet ourselves down. It is a prayer of silence, a prayer of surrender. We pray for nothing; we hope for nothing. Our prayer is our communion with the nothingness of God. In communion with God, we come to hope God's hope. When we pray, "Our Father, who art in heaven, hallowed be your name. Your kingdom come, your will be done on earth as it is in heaven," we are saying, "I hope, not for what I hope, but for what you hope. Your way is the way I choose." We love God and God loves us. Our love gives us the faith to believe in God as the only power to which we will yield. As we become one with God we live God's love, live God's life, and hope God's hope. Scripture says that "There are in the end three things that last: faith,

hope, and love, and the greatest of these is love"
(1 Cor 13:13). This is because faith and hope both
come from love.

We do not understand life as God does, so we cannot really hope for one thing over another. To hope for
nothing is to hope in God. When our hope is in God
alone, we are free from hoping for anything else. That
in which we hope is that to which we give our heart.
Jesus warned those who would listen: "Do not lay up
for yourselves an earthly treasure. Moths and rust corrode; thieves break in and steal. Make it your practice
instead to store up heavenly treasure, which neither
moths nor rust corrode nor thieves break in and steal.
Remember, where your treasure is, there your heart is
also" (Mt 6:19). Above all, our soul craves for God
and all that is God; our heart yearns for God, a God
that is intimate, a God that can be known only
through love. What is our purpose in this life if not to
love and serve God?

God helps us to look beyond the mundane and the
temporal toward that which matters most. God helps
us to hold fast to that which cannot be pilfered,
eroded, or lost, and to cling to that which is rooted in
the deepest soil of our heart, and transcends the lim-
its of our life. What we come to cherish is what pre-
occupies our mind and spirit.

Our consciousness is the light of our soul. If it
emanates from God, the light will illuminate our soul,
if the light is diluted by anything other than God, our
soul will be in darkness. We must choose. We cannot

have God and at the same time embrace that which keeps us apart from God. Loving God and doing God's will must be our only purpose. We cannot go in two directions. When we divide our intentions we scatter the forces of our soul. We must obsess on God and let this magnificent obsession take precedence over all other obsessions.

We must give ourselves totally to God and let even the basic necessities of life become secondary. We must preserve our life and provide for ourselves that which is essential for healthy living. Hope enables us to die to the old that the new may live. Inordinate preoccupation with anything material will turn us away from the light. Our life is of more value than that which sustains it, and we are more dear than that which protects us.

We must discover our essence as God's children, intent, not on the mechanics of living, but on the meaning of life. We must rest in the hope that God knows us better than we know ourselves, and that all we really need is already ours. Let nothing be more important to us than loving God. Let nothing stand in the way of following God's will. Let our heart be filled with hope in God, let our mind be filled with thoughts of God, and let our hands be filled with work for God. Hope is not future oriented, but focused on the now. If we cannot hope in the present moment where life happens, then we cannot hope at all. Our hope is in the possibility of the moment before us. It is in the now that we reach the fullness of our humanity. It is in the now that we listen to the will of God and re-spond with all our soul. We must be willing to stay in the present moment where love abides. Tomorrow will be affected by what we do with today. As we live fully the moment before us, and dare to stay with God, our preoccupation with anything else will fade away. It is in the now that God touches our soul and awakens it from slumber. The awakened soul hopes.

In the Midst of Winter

God, there is a part of me that dies in winter. The winds of life strip my defenses, and hopelessness stills my spirit. This is the time of my barren heart.

In the midst of winter I am left with nothing of myself. My plans have gone awry, and my ways no longer work. The winter sun grows darker, and the shadows overtake me. I am naked and exposed and I have no place to hide.

In the midst of winter I am tempted to despair. All seems futile, all appears lost. I am tired of the struggle, and I do not dare to hope. The future looks bleak and the choices are few. I can choose a life of death or I can die to myself that I may live.

In the midst of winter the external falls away. There is nothing left to do but to go within and wait. My instinct is to search for the nourishment that will sustain me, and I seek it deep within. Preserved in the depths of my being is all that I need to make it through this season of fruitlessness. There, hidden from my prideful self, is the one who will tend me through the night. There, at the core of who I am, I discover who you are, God.

Why does it take a winter to bring me back to you? Why must I be emptied before I can be filled? Why must I be wounded before I can be healed? Why must I be lost before I can be found? Can there be the spring without the winter? Can there be the union without the separation?

In the midst of winter my pace is slowed. I am compelled to stop and wait. My patience grows and my faith is tested. In the midst of winter I have the need to pray and the time to listen. My eyes are closed and I begin to see. The superfluous is left behind. In the midst of winter there is nothing left but love.

In the midst of winter, when my reasons to live have faded away, your reason for life is set before me. When I have nothing left to lose, I gain back my soul. In the midst of winter I am left hopeless, yet it is here that I find my hope in you.

9

Life in Balance

LIFE IS STRESSFUL and it will always be stressful. When we least expect it, we are torn from our quiet place and thrown into the strife. And, when we least expect it, we discover the eye of the storm in the midst of the tornado. This is the nature of life and it is not within our power to alter the nature of life. It is, however, within our power to decide how we will respond to that stressful life. It is our responsibility to deal with life as it is, and yet, to do so from who we truly are — children of God. Even in the hell of a stressful life, the spirit within us responds with the serenity of heaven.

Having Faith

Sometimes it may seem as though the whole world is falling down on us. It is as though everything is going wrong all at once. Our life is in trouble and we do not know where to turn.

These times of anguish are also times of despair. It is in the midst of our troubles that we feel the urge to run away, to check out, to put our mind on hold, or even to cease existing in hope that the pain of living will disappear. We wonder how much more we can take before we crack.

The twisting knot in our chest and the draining tension in our head are real to us. Words about having faith tend to sound empty and unreal at times like these. Considering heavenly things or comparing our state of life with the glory of eternal life doesn't really help us. We need practical help based on the nature of our humanity, and on our grounded faith in God.

But having faith during the onslaught of trouble does not mean believing in God as a rescuer. It doesn't mean that we are to ask God for extra help to get through our difficult times. Having faith in God means believing that God has already given us all that we need to confront the adversities of life.

One such gift is the ability to divide and conquer the crises which come our way. When we forget to use this gift, we allow too much stimuli — too many problems to enter our consciousness and overwhelm us. Our greatest temptation is to despair in the face of what appears to be more than we can handle.

Tomorrow will take care of itself. Our focus must be on what is before us today, right now. In this way we break down the seemingly insurmountable into portions which we are equipped to handle mentally, emotionally, physically, and spiritually. If we allow all of our problems and all of their possible consequences to inundate us all at once, we short-circuit and become immobilized. We render ourselves incapable of coping at all. But when we scale down the crisis to fit our abilities, we are able to cope. Instead of the year, we consider only the moment; instead of the staircase, we consider only the step; instead of the problem, we consider only a part of the problem.

Another gift is the ability to slay the phantoms of the past and future, and to focus on the present moment and all that we can bring to it. In the final analysis, the present moment is all that is given to us, and living it effectively is all that is expected of us. When we can focus in this way, we tap a tremendous reservoir of human capabilities. We gain the composure necessary to make the appropriate decisions; we become aware of our emotions, such as fear and anxiety, and express them without falling victim to them; and we experience a surge of energy that fuels our body according to our need.

The faith that we must have, especially when we are in trouble, is not in what God can do to save us, but in what God has already done. Our faith must be in the effectiveness of the tools which God has provided.

Our faith must be in the power of the present moment. Our faith must be in ourselves, who are capable of living as children of God, even in crisis.

Releasing Control

The purpose of our spirituality is not to gain complete control over our life, but to surrender it to the love and mercy of God. But we may not want to surrender control because we believe that we need it in order to protect ourselves from harm.

Perhaps we grew up in a troubled home and control has been our defense against a cruel and unpredictable world. We may believe that the more control we have, the safer we will be. Perhaps we were overly controlled in the past, or we were traumatized or humiliated. Maybe we were a victim of physical, sexual or emotional abuse. In any case, the logic we adopted was that control would keep this from happening to us again.

We may try to control by becoming very rigid in our way of life. We lose all flexibility and spontaneity and, instead, we regulate our every action to ensure predictability about what happens to us. We may have learned to control our feelings. We may suppress our emotions because we fear that to express them openly will leave us vulnerable to others. The danger here is that suppressed feelings will not remain suppressed and will surface in destructive ways. We may become depressed, physically sick, or we may explode emotionally.

Actually, the stress we experience is not due to the circumstances we face, but to our fear of not being able to control them, so our attempts to control just bring on more stress.

Our control may go beyond ourselves to others. We may believe that the best defense is a good offense, so we attempt to control others before they control us. We may reason that if controlling our own life keeps us safe, then controlling the lives of others will keep them safe too. In fact, by controlling we end up hurting others more than helping them.

The issue of control is a real paradox. The more control we try to grasp, the less we have. The more control we surrender to God, the more under control our life becomes. But surrendering control doesn't mean becoming passive or fatalistic. It means that we trust that God has equipped us with the physical, emotional, and spiritual tools necessary to negotiate life. To surrender control to God means to release the tension within that keeps us from responding to life with our full capacity.

Accepting Imperfection

God loves us unconditionally just as we are at this moment.

We were created and are being created at the same

time. We are in transition, moving through a process of growth and learning, a process that never ends. We must not judge ourselves at any given point of our life, instead, we are to accept our incompleteness and forgive our imperfection.

Our temptation is to despair over our slow progress and to judge it as insufficient and unacceptable. To be human is to be in the process of becoming. Rather than be disappointed or shamed at the sight of our imperfection, we affirm ourselves for the progress we have made, however small, and are hopeful of what is yet to come.

As we acknowledge that we are in transition, we become mindful that others are also in transition and are in need of our patience and understanding. This does not mean that we must allow the ways of others to hurt us, but that we may allow them the time and opportunity to keep growing and changing. We can forgive others their imperfections at the same time that we protect ourselves from their hurtful behavior. We can let others know how they affect us even as we encourage them to persevere in the process of their growth.

To seek a perfect world is to sentence ourselves to a life of disillusion and frustration. To embrace an imperfect world is to allow for the spirit of God to move through us and to make a difference in the process. We cannot wait until we are perfect to love ourselves, and we cannot wait for others to be perfect before we can love them. Love must happen now.

Being Who We Are

We must be who we are, nothing more, nothing less. Let us enter into the part of us that holds the treasure of our innermost self. Let us behold the real us, and dare to stay there, unmasked, naked and vulnerable, grounded in the reality of our true and authentic being.

Let us release our desire for external approval. Let it fall away along with the masks we wear for others. The false us has to do with the needs and expectations of those who do not know who we really are. We must allow the false us to grow smaller as our more authentic self grows larger. See the false trappings fall away from us like a serpent shedding its skin. Feel the essence of our being emerge from its hidden place and enter into the light.

Perhaps it was necessary to portray a different self in the beginning. Maybe it was the only way to survive the treacherous passageways of life. But now it is time to set aside that which is not ours. Now it is time to let ourselves be all that we are.

We are dark; we are light; we are whole. We are creative; we are destructive; we are whole. We are open; we are closed; we are whole. We are broken; we are mended; we are whole. We are perfect; we are imperfect; we are whole.

There will be those who will approve of us and those who will not. There will be those who will love us and those who will not. The only thing that really matters is that we are accepted and loved by God, now and forever, and that we are loved by ourselves, just as we are.

Let us enter into the freedom of spontaneity. Let us surrender the control of our environment. Let us end our obsession with our image. Let ourselves just be. We are the dawning of a new day, unencumbered by the clouds of make-believe. We are the rediscovery of a secret garden that has been there from the beginning.

Listening to Ourselves

Let us listen to the voice of life. It reveals to us the secrets of our nature. It tells us the truth to which we must respond.

Let us listen to the pleading of our body. It is racked with pain and twisted by tension. It is wounded by disease and broken by neglect. It asks for rest and relaxation for it is weary from overwork and under-play. It asks to be touched and it asks to be healed. We hear its scream to stop the abuse. We hear it cry for tender care and loving attention. Let us listen to the voice of our physical selves.

Listen to the whispers of the mind. We can hear them only if we ignore the intrusion of vagabond thoughts and the distractions of wild imaginings. We hear the voice that comes from the reservoir of all experience and knowledge; of all the past and possibility. This is the voice that will guide us through the desert. It will tell us what works best for us, and it will help us set priorities. This is the voice that will help us make decisions all the moments of our life, but we must heed its words. We listen to the voice of our mind, for it is the source of the gift we leave this world. Its prompting will feed our creativity and its questions will eat of the fruit of the yet unknown.

Listen to the music of our heart. Its notes are sweet and gentle, harsh and explosive. Its range is from high and ecstatic to low and depressive. Its melody is sometimes sad and at other times pregnant with the joy of heaven. The music of our heart sings the song of our emotions. Its lyrics tell us how we are responding to the reality of life. We listen to the words, listen to the music, know what we are feeling and sing it to another. We do not critique the music of our heart, we just let it be heard.

Listen to the silence of our soul. It is here that our whole self can rest in unconditional acceptance and nurturing love. Here the quest for knowing gives way to the security of believing. Here is where our scattered emotions settle into the peace of oneness. We listen to the silence of our soul. It invites us to integrate the world of our body, mind, and heart into the wholeness of God. It tells us that it is through the totality of our humanity that we transcend it. Amid the silence of our soul we will hear the still small voice of God.

Being Reconciled

It is not enough to resist killing our enemy; the resentment we hold against him imprisons us in the hell of a deadened life.

To feel anger against another because he has hurt us is natural and healthy, to remain stuck in the anger forever is stifling and disintegrating. Whatever separates us from another also separates us from ourselves because, at our innermost we are one.

To be reconciled with those from whom we are alienated we must first reconcile the alienated parts of ourselves. To be reconciled does not necessarily mean to befriend or to reconnect. Rather, it means that the issue that divides us from another must be dealt with and resolved, at least within ourselves. It may or may not include external manifestation of the reconciliation.

The road toward reconciliation is not paved with denial or suppression of the issues at hand. It is forged through the difficult terrain of confrontation, forgiveness and integration. The road toward reconciliation is impossible to travel alone. Only through our complete dependence on the grace of the God within us can we find the courage and the perseverance to traverse it to the end.

We must remove from ourselves the part that is poisoning us, the part that is toxic to the whole. We must expurgate from within us anything that works against our integration. God is our truest self. Let nothing stand in the way of God.

Allowing Simplicity

How are we to be simple in a world that is becoming more complex by the minute? How are we to simplify when our state in life demands so much from us? Is there something we can do to become simple? Do we need to sell our possessions, quit our job, go off into the desert? Do we have to grow our own food, change the clothes we wear, stop learning?

No external action on our part will result in simplicity. No particular lifestyle or socioeconomic state will ensure simplicity. Simplicity imposed from without is tantamount to legalism. Simplicity is a state of mind. It is the consequence of how we live our moments internally. Even simplicity, when seen as a virtue and pursued for its own sake, becomes just another object of our ambition, and in our pursuit of it we chase it away.

The word "simplicity" comes from the Latin "simplus," meaning "single," or "one," yet life is, for the most part, riddled with duplicity. We are diminished by going in too many directions at the same time, by not deciding what is the most important thing and living accordingly.

In almost every case of conflict or complication we discover that we either do not know what is essential to us, or we are confusing the secondary with the essential. The bondage of our duplicity comes when we have not chosen among competing attachments what we hold above all others. The inward focus on the one thing necessary brings freedom from the chains of anxiety. It also brings peace and unity to our external living.

Our internal focus on God calls us to a radical obedience to the sovereign of our life. We obey God when we obey the laws of nature, including physical, psychological, and spiritual laws. We obey God when we hold God hallowed above all else and love God with all of our being.

Our internal focus on God reveals to us how total our dependence is on God. We depend on God for the very faith to depend on God. We depend on God for the daily bread that nourishes us through the physical, emotional and psychological famines of life. We depend on God for the drink of living water that sustains us through the drought of the soul. When we hunger and thirst for communion with God, then nothing else is as important — nothing!

The renouncement of the external, whether it be wealth, the opinion of others, or an addiction, does not, in and of itself, bring us simplicity, but our surrender to God detaches us from all the rest to the extent that we can put it into perspective and manage it effectively.

The internal focus on God affects the way we think,

feel, and act. Our single eye on God affects the decisions we make about possessions, relationships, and lifestyles. We become simple from the inside out.

Receiving the Gift of Time

Time is a river that flows through the ages. We cannot stop it, but merely change its course; we cannot possess it, only use it well. The water that passes us right now is the present moment, the river is eternity.

Time is an illusion. In an effort to control it, it has been measured out in seconds, decades, and millenniums, but time has no beginning and it has no end. It will not be captured in a segment and it will not be broken down.

Of course, we must contend with clocks and calendars lest we fall into chaos and disorientation, but the attitude we take toward time determines whether it is an opportunity to use or a master to serve.

Time is a gift to us from God. What we do with it is our gift to God. When we live our moments trying to meet our high expectations of productivity and achievement, we may be responding to our need for approval, acceptance and love. When we come to believe that we are already unconditionally approved of, accepted and loved by God, we can allow ourselves to enjoy God's gift of time not only working, but playing, walking, learning, crying, laughing, dancing, praying, or just doing nothing. Maybe God's pleasure comes when we use our gift of time to live fully and spontaneously.

We can misuse our gift of time. We may be hounded by the passing of time because we are so preoccupied about not wasting it. An attempt to hoard our time like a miser is a sure step toward wasting it. In our greed and anxiety about time we may become immobilized and bring about the very result we fear so much. When we let time be free, we also free ourselves internally to what we must do.

We sometimes blame time for our own inaction? We may conclude that we don't have time for something or someone. In reality, what we don't have are priorities. The time is always there, what we choose to do with it is another matter.

Time is neutral. We attribute power to it that it does not have. We may have heard it said that "time heals." But time does not heal. It is what we do or do not do as time passes that does the healing. In this same way, it is what we choose to do with our time that determines the nature of our life. We may talk about spending time, wasting time, giving time, taking time, killing time, and so on, but what we really do is make choices every moment about what to do with our life.

Like any precious gift, our time must be appreciated, used appropriately, and enjoyed in the present. In obsessing about past or future time, we lose the moment before us. It is in the moment that we can make a difference. In a moment we can divert disaster; in a moment we can choose to live or die; in a moment we can repent; in a moment we can love.

We must focus on the moment, not on its limitations. Let us frame our life in the spirit of everlasting time. Let us realize that this moment is in eternity, and that eternity is in this moment.

Keeping the Sabbath

To keep the Sabbath means much more than just following the dictates of church law. It means more than disciplining ourselves to go to church on Sunday or synagogue on Saturday. To honor the Sabbath means that we love and honor ourselves.

We are invited to stop in the course of our daily living and take time for what is most important to us — ourselves and our relationships with God and others. To keep the Sabbath means that we acknowledge our basic need to reconnect with God regularly and frequently. It means that we admit to ourselves that we cannot live and move and work in the world for very long without returning to the source of all life in order to be restored. It means that we humbly allow the rest that our soul requires if we are to continue to serve God in the world.

In Hebrew, "Sabbath" means "a time of rest," and "rest" means freedom from activity or labor. Even God "rested on the seventh day from all the work he had undertaken" (Genesis 2:2). Rest is imperative in the work of creation and co-creation. It is the space between bursts of energy; it is the silence between words spoken; it is the death between times of living.

We are called to keep the Sabbath because without stopping to rest, to gather ourselves, and to remember who we are, we will live without purpose, direction, or meaning. Stopping to rest on the Sabbath, regardless of what day of the week we choose to do it, breaks us out of our routine and brings us to a level of consciousness that we do not usually enjoy in our everyday living.

How we spend the moments of our Sabbath depends on us. Perhaps we need physical rest more than anything else. Perhaps we find ourselves wanting to learn, perhaps we need to express our feelings with a friend. We may need community or we may need aloneness. One need that is constant is our need to pray — to communicate with God heart to heart. Probably we will need to do some of all of these.

Entering the Silence

Imagine being quiet, even for a moment. What a helpless feeling if we use words to control and manipulate the world around us. What vulnerability if we prefer to hide behind chatter and clatter, lest we be left alone with God.

Silence may threaten our very existence because we have identified being with noise and activity for too long. By allowing silence to envelop us in the midst of the noise, we surrender to the activity of God, and we become receptive to what God wants to give us. We touch upon the reality that goes beyond the senses.

The noises that have our attention are not limited to those that we hear through our ears. We are also plagued with psychic disturbances, wounded memories, anxious thoughts, and the loneliness that comes from a meaningless life. Even our futile and presumptuous attempts to understand God are the noises of the mind that drown out the silence of the heart.

To go beyond our habitual consciousness we must move toward the center of our heart and embrace the God who dwells there. It may seem like emptiness to us in the beginning, but in the desert of our heart is pure being in which we are given a deeper awareness of hidden things. In our silence of the mind we no longer seek revelation. We are merely receptive and revelation comes.

We must be careful to attend to our body as we become silent. There must be a letting go of our physical being that allows integration and centeredness. We need to be physically relaxed and we need a quiet place to wait for God. We need to stay in the present moment and from there we enter a tranquil state of loving surrender.

Our spirituality, our prayer, becomes not a speaking, but a listening. We move from communication with God to communion with God. We are held there in moments of deep absorption in the Whole. The prayer of the heart is silent because the language of the soul is love.

Putting on the Yoke of Love

Come to the God within, you who are tired and weary, you who are overwhelmed and overburdened.

Here you will find rest, here you will be refreshed.

Let yourself be soothed and nurtured by the mothering of God.

Let yourself go, release the tension of the day and the stress that overcomes you.

Close your eyes and be in the moment.

Receive the grace that comes.

You work so hard, you carry great responsibility, and you are weighed down with the problems of the world.

You are bent over with the heaviness of life.

Come to the God within.

Here you will unload all that you have taken upon yourself; here you will shoulder the yoke of love.

Come to the God within, not so that God can help, but that you can help God.

Release your hold on the reins of control, and surrender to the yoke of love.

Here you do not work alone, but with God who also wears the yoke.

Release your conception of a God of power whose mighty hand will set things right.

Learn from God the ways of love.

Let yourself be gentle. Nothing good comes through force.

Let yourself be humble. Your strength lies in your truthfulness with self.

Listen to the rhythm of God's heart.

The anxious, rapid beating of your heart gives way to the slow and steady, strong and loving pulsation of God.

Come to the God within and you will find rest for your soul, for with God the yoke of love is easy and the burden of life is light.

Published by Resurrection Press

A Rachel Rosary Larry Kupferman	$4.50
Blessings All Around Us Dolores Leckey	$8.95
Catholic Is Wonderful Mitch Finley	$4.95
Christian Marriage John & Therese Boucher	$4.95
Come, Celebrate Jesus! Francis X. Gaeta	$4.95
From Holy Hour to Happy Hour Francis X. Gaeta	$7.95
Glory to Glory Francis Clare, SSND	$10.95
Healing through the Mass Robert DeGrandis, SSJ	$8.95
Healing the Wounds of Emotional Abuse Nancy Benvenga	$6.95
Healing Your Grief Ruthann Williams, OP	$7.95
Life, Love and Laughter Jim Vlaun	$7.95
Living Each Day by the Power of Faith Barbara Ryan	$8.95
The Joy of Being a Catechist Gloria Durka	$4.95
The Joy of Being a Eucharistic Minister Mitch Finley	$5.95
Transformed by Love Margaret Magdalen, CSMV	$5.95
RVC Liturgical Series: The Liturgy of the Hours	$3.95
The Lector's Ministry	$3.95
Behold the Man Judy Marley, SFO	$4.50
Loving Yourself for God's Sake Adolfo Quezada	$5.95
Mustard Seeds Matthew Kelly	$7.95
Practicing the Prayer of Presence van Kaam/Muto	$8.95
5-Minute Miracles Linda Schubert	$4.95
Season of New Beginnings Mitch Finley	$4.95
Season of Promises Mitch Finley	$4.95
Soup Pot Ethel Pochocki	$8.95
Stay with Us John Mullin, SJ	$3.95
Surprising Mary Mitch Finley	$7.95
Teaching as Eucharist Joanmarie Smith	$5.95
The Healing Rosary Mike D.	$5.95
What He Did for Love Francis X. Gaeta	$5.95
You Are My Beloved Mitch Finley	$10.95
Your Sacred Story Robert Lauder	$6.95
Your Wounds I Will Heal Faricy / Rooney	$8.95

For a free catalog call 1-800-892-6657